THE VERY BEST BAD IDEA

INNOVATION, CREATIVITY, AND MAKING FRIENDS WITH THE MOUSE

KIRK WESTWOOD

NEW DEGREE PRESS

THE VERY BEST BAD IDEA

Innovation, Creativity, andMaking Friends with the Mouse

ISBN

978-1-64137-523-8   *Paperback*

978-1-64137-524-5   *Kindle Ebook*

978-1-64137-525-2   *Digital Ebook*

To

Peace, Strength, and Victory
the Perfect Musical Force
a Lily of the Valley
and the Watchtower of course

A Lion in the Garden
A Mother with her Fold
Initiatives Assembled
that these stories can be told

A life lived in fear is a life half-lived.

—BAZ LUHRMANN

CONTENTS

——

YOU'RE DOING THAT WRONG

———

"That's not how this works."
"You're doing this all wrong."
"Don't reinvent the WHEEL!"
"You have to do it THIS way."
"That is a TERRIBLE idea!"

—TESTAMENTS OF A JOB WELL DONE (PROBABLY).

LET'S TAKE THIS FROM THE TOP

The world is a pretty screwy place. (I'd like to say that in a far more colorful manner, but frankly my mom will probably read this book, so we are going to endeavor to keep it PG-13. Hi, Mom.)

As a population, we cling to ideas we hate, fear things that are benign, embrace stuff that will actually kill us, and as a whole, obsess over reality TV (not sure if this last point is relevant, but it certainly goes to my "world is a screwy place" concept so … let's roll with it).

We claim to crave innovation while often being utterly punishing to those who dare try to innovate. We conflate, confuse, and contradict terms with other ones, making effective communication more or less impossible. We standardize our education system to mandate the process of getting the answer, not the ability to do so. We reward all participants to dull the pain of the "loser," and in doing so we effectively eliminate the reward for the "winner."

Even the so-called "innovation" companies that flood the beltway in the D.C. area, or thread through Silicon Valley, tend to wrap themselves up in rigid systems and policies. Bureaucracies and self-imposed limitations effectively strangle what they insist on calling "innovation"—a buzz word they don't seem to understand.

Statements ring out like "unlocking innovation" or "disrupting industries," when what they tend to mean is: "We build gadgets, widgets, and tech that you never knew you wanted."

We have access to more information at faster speeds than we have at any point in history … so how is it that we find the truth harder to reach? A baseline of understanding more or less impossible?

The 1948 Nobel Prize winner, T.S. Eliot, said in his play "The Rock"[1]:

> *Where is the wisdom we have lost in knowledge?*
> *Where is the knowledge we have lost in information?*[1]

... and HERE's the issue.

Our schools teach a rigid system structured around finding a solution to—not an understanding of—the problem.

"Children! SHOW YOUR WORK!"

Society favors the best followers, best employees, best students, and those who work best within the system. We only really herald the outliers of success and punish those who dare try and fail for ever daring to step out of line.

"KNOW YOUR PLACE!"

We tell children they can accomplish *"anything"* ... then tell them what THEY want to accomplish.

Teacher: *You can be anything! An astronaut, a doctor, a lawyer, THE PRESIDENT!*

Student: *I want to restore and service vintage cars!*
Teacher: *Ugh, a mechanic?! Aim higher! You can be anything!*

---

1   Eliot, T. S. (1934), The Rock, p.1 London: Faber & Faber.

Student: *But ... I really love engines and working with my hands.*

Teacher: *You are selling yourself short! You'll never be really successful as just a mechanic!*

Somewhere along the way, wealth became the prime goal and money the universal scorekeeper. But we lost sight of where wealth comes from.

Peter Drucker, the Austrian-born entrepreneur and management consultant often lauded as "*The Father of Modern Management*," said it best:

> "*We know now that the source of wealth is something specifically human: Knowledge.*
>
> *If we apply knowledge to tasks we already know how to do, we call it 'productivity.'*
>
> *If we apply knowledge to tasks that are new and different, we call it 'innovation.'*
>
> *Only knowledge allows us to achieve these two goals.*"[2]

If I might deign to throw my two cents in with T.S. Eliot and Peter Drucker, we have been leaving out perspective.

---

2   Peter Drucker "Landmarks of Tomorrow" 1959 p263

If knowledge is the pinnacle of wealth and in many ways the cornerstone of humanity, a single piece of information, equipped with the knowledge of three equally intelligent people and strained through their individual perspective, will often yield three significantly different nuggets of wisdom.

Jack Ma, former CEO of the Alibaba Group and noted Chinese billionaire business phenom and philanthropist, said what has become one of my favorite quotes about perspective:

"Intelligent people need a fool to lead them. When the team's all a bunch of scientists, it is best to have a peasant lead the way. His way of thinking is different. It's easier to win if you have people seeing things from different perspectives."[3]
Knowledge, wisdom, information, innovation can all easily be trumped by a fool's perspective.

FOR TODAY, I'M YOUR FOOL

My perspective isn't anything special; it just happens to be mine. I was in my thirties before I realized that my difficulty in school, social awkwardness, failure to work in certain environments, and paradoxical relationship with authority all stemmed from one common source—my general world outlook was "wrong."

I have a weird relationship with social cues. I've been told I read people fairly well, and I try to emulate common behaviors

---

3   Caroline Frost, "Jack Ma, the Richest Man in China, Stepped Down as
     Alibaba Chairman," 2019 Markets Insider

in most situations, but I have difficulty being "myself." I've come to understand that this struggle reads as awkward, or even intimidating in certain situations.

My lifelong study of communications, facial tics, body language, and both verbal and nonverbal cues has served me particularly well at operating within most social structures. However, I have also struggled my entire life with feeling "comfortable" or "at home" almost anywhere. I survived in part through emulation and striving to make myself a giant mirror. I don't have what others often refer to as a "self-identity."

Due to an adolescent established passion for films, a round of film school, and some hard time in Tinseltown, I've seen in excess of 15,000 movies in my life. To that end, much of my social programming came from film. I pick the character who fits a situation ... and I go for it.

I "medicated" my awkwardness with catharsis.

As a military brat, I moved constantly and never found ground with a particular group of friends or social structure. I learned everything I needed to know about groups of friends from The *Sandlot, Stand by Me, The Goonies, and Hook.*

For my entire young life, I assumed my perspectives, the way I processed information, and the way I had movies and media playing in my head twenty-three hours and forty-five minutes a day were just how it was for everyone.

But I have since been assured that I actually see situations a bit differently from other people. My brain is nothing special nor noteworthy; I just process information a little differently—my perspective is "off."

In fact, I consistently struggle to see situations as "the group" describes. I see odd logical fallacies and irrationality in the status quo, but there's a remarkably good chance you do too.

I see humor and inconvenience where others seem to see unsurpassable problems. To colleagues' and coworkers' chagrin or at least annoyance, I see success where they see failure, and most significantly, I sometimes see FAILURE where they see SUCCESS.

As much as I've tried to fit in, I find that more often than not *I'm the fool surrounded by scientists.*

WHERE ARE WE GOING ...
AND WHAT'S WITH THE HANDBASKET?
We were taught, trained, and indoctrinated by people who meant well ... but didn't know.

Our companies, corporations, and government use data from one set of results and proudly apply it to unrelated principles. We show deference to systems put in place long ago by our wizened progenitors for reasons we deign not question lest ... we ... be ... punished ... or ...

I don't know! But people seem to think questioning the systems is really bad, so stop it or ... again, I'm not sure the consequences, but I'm promised that some exist.

Society defines success for us, despite the fact that success is completely subjective, relatively ineffable, basically unconformable, and completely distinct for each individual. Benchmarks, touchpoints, and grades are culturally assigned as a way of standardizing education, success, and progress, despite the fact that, again, education, success, and progress are ultimately unstandardizable (← let's pretend that's a word).

WHICH LEADS US TO ...
If something doesn't look, sound, or feel right, it must be wrong ... even if it works ... even if it works better ... even if it makes far more sense, is less expensive, easier to do, and more or less right, it has to be comfortable or it's wrong.

It has to look like how we used to do it.

If it doesn't ... there are consequences ...

... ghosts, *or something* ...

No one has been able to really tell me what will happen if we break with tradition, but the outcome must be really bad.

A friend recently told me something that spoke very plainly to this:

"Tradition is just peer pressure from dead people."

I'm here to add my Nancy Reagan to the mix:

"Just Say No."

I FIGURED IT OUT:

My perspective might be "off." I very much might see the world "wrong." But I don't think I'm nearly as alone as I've been led to believe. A lot of us are "weird." But we shouldn't care that we are. We don't have the time to conform to someone else's definition of success.

We shouldn't spend the energy striving for the outcome WE are looking for in a form that is more easily recognizable to other people.

There isn't nearly enough *"give-a-damn"* (← real noun)

to have us pass by our own goals to meet the goals that our dearly departed forefathers in all their apparent wisdom laid out for us decades in advance.

I don't want to ruffle feathers just to ruffle feathers.

But I want to do the best I CAN. Not the best someone else can do by having me do their job.

I FOUND A SECRET, THE SIGNAL, SOME SIGNIFICANCE.
This notion sounds definitively counterintuitive, but I discovered that when someone criticized an idea by either referencing its nonconformity or being unable to specify why exactly it was "wrong," the reason was because it wasn't.

It just activated some deeply rooted social programming they probably didn't know they were perpetuating. So, let's talk about how some of these criticisms really translate:

"That's not how this works!" This expression is a great signal that you might have found an opportunity.

"You're doing this wrong!" This statement begs far more questions than it does adequately signal an incorrect action.

"That's a terrible idea!" This one is my favorite, as unless the person actually thinks you're an idiot, this statement is the best to indicate you've discovered a radical transformation. (If they DO think you're an idiot, this is a cast-the-gauntlet type of opportunity.)

My next statement is going to sound glib and fairly incomplete, but as that's what the rest of the book is for, I promise to explain:

The person who encourages, cultivates, and fosters your
"bad ideas"
is the person who wants to see you succeed.

The more I told people my discovery that "bad ideas" are good, and good ideas are forgettable, the more I found people were either excitedly activated with the possibilities, or inexplicably and disproportionately negative and unwilling to even hear any matter of explanation.

As a remarkably obsessive individual, that reaction kept me up nights. *(Full disclosure: I'm an insomniac—I was already up at night, so this just gave me something productive to do.)*

And so I began my multiyear journey that became this book; I'd like to take you down my favorite paths:

PART 1—The History of Thinking: We'll start at the beginning of society and discuss the concepts of conformity, evolution, neuroscience, and memory, just so we have the same baseline.

PART 2—Make Friends with the Mouse: We'll tear apart innovation vs. invention and show that IDEAS, KNOWLEDGE, PROCESS, and PERSPECTIVES are the truest forms of wealth, and money is just a byproduct.

PART 3—Release the Kreative: We'll unwrap the idea that the biggest obstacle standing in your way is you, running programming you didn't know you had. Fact of the matter is: you are brilliant.

That isn't a platitude or a "special snowflake" statement. You are brilliant, or you could be ...

But our culture standardized us, our brain is betraying us, and our family is lying to us.

If we *Release the Kreative,* we find our way home.

PERFECT ... ANOTHER BOOK ON "NONCONFORMITY"
No. Not directly.

One of my top-five favorite thought leaders and authors is Adam Grant. His book *Originals: How Nonconformists Move the World* helped me understand a lot about myself.

In his book, Grant demonstrates and uses a great deal of academic research to talk about "Originals" in the third person—like Jane Goodall about chimpanzees, or Dian Fossey of Gorillas in the Mist. He does phenomenal work to unpack and dissect what makes a nonconformist "tick," from an outside, anthropological standpoint.

Originals is one of my all-time favorite books, and the admiration and respect I have for Adam Grant knows no bounds. But where Originals "fails" is in identifying how to navigate a world of nonconformity when you aren't choosing to be one.

I'm on the right track, baby
I was born this way
—LADY GAGA, "BORN THIS WAY"

Originals explains nonconformists and empowers nonconformists to be such. But it acts as a guide to navigating nonconformity, by expressing its merits. It doesn't as much guide a person who isn't trying to buck the system, but rather honestly doesn't see the system, understand the system, or agree with the system.

Nonconformity is most often disregarded as a defiant choice. A decision to kick against the norms. However, if anything, conformity is kicking against one's intelligence, perspective, and personal beliefs, all out of fear of losing "the group."

This isn't a book about "nonconformists" nor would I classify myself AS one.

It's about conformity ... and why we care.

After three years passively researching and seeking to understand, I dove deep to dissect this concept. I spent a year researching innovators, creatives, disruptors, philosophers, and academics. I interviewed people who broke paradigms, changed industries, rebelled against the standard, and most of them did so with ideas, simply changing the way they looked at a problem.

I am not an anthropologist, psychologist, sociologist, or any other such "-ist" that would give me any particular credential, which is why I called every expert with a phone number to make sure I wasn't crazy before I wrote this book.

They couldn't assure me of my sanity, but I left each conversation with a fair amount of confidence in my data and insight, as it is not my data, and I had my insight checked by people who are smarter than me for a living.

"I'm not crazy; my mother had me tested."

—SHELDON, THE BIG BANG THEORY

This book is an account of having a unique perspective on something, like you do. This book acknowledges and dissects the myth of the way it's done.

This book gives you permission for what you never needed permission for: to have an opinion, to be noticed, to challenge the right way, and to recognize recognition when it matters.

This book makes no apologies for irreverence nor self-reference, and more than anything, this book challenges the statement "That's not how this works" with the simple question: "According to whom?"

PART ONE

THE HISTORY OF THINKING

CHAPTER ONE

HISTORY 001

———

**THE STORIES MY PROFESSORS THOUGHT WERE IMPORTANT
TOLD IN A WAY THAT PROVES THEIR POINT
TESTED ON TO ASSURE I SAW THINGS THEIR WAY**

*TL;DR—Human fear is a byproduct of millennia of evolution in
response to common risks. Humans' greatest strength is within
society. Losing society historically ended in death. Conclusion:
Modern people often fear standing out or looking stupid with
the same biological response as death.*

I hate bees. Truly. I have gotten better over the years, but
people who have been around me and an errant bee have
seen what could be described as visceral, soul-shaking fear,
and panicking anxiety. For as long as I can remember, bees
have affected me beyond my control.

No, I am not allergic.
Yes, I have been stung.
No, I don't think it hurts that bad.

Yes, it is in fact a remarkably mild annoyance. But the fact remains that I am terrified of bees.

My mom hates snakes. Her hatred of snakes makes my aversion of bees look like a passing dislike. As a child my mom could not be in a house if she knew it contained a pet snake. She told my brothers and me fairly often that when we grew up, if we didn't want her to visit, we had a simple solution: get a snake.

My mom's fear of snakes, whilst perhaps a bit overdramatic, is a remarkably common fear, despite the fact that dying by snake bite in the United States is less likely than being struck by lightning.[4]

People fear the dark, while sitting in hermetically sealed houses, which would have been considered a near fortress in previous eras. Another prevalent fear is that of spiders—if you are curious, average annual fatalities in the United States due to spider bites is 6.6. Conversely, deaths by household dog attack average thirty-one,[4] but dogs are cute … so that number isn't relevant.

Car crashes kill tens of thousands of people each year. Of these, nearly 50 percent of fatalities in motor accidents happen because passengers weren't using a readily accessible, legally required precaution: their seatbelts.[5]

---

4   "Venomous Snake FAQs." 2020. Ufwildlife.Ifas.Ufl.Edu.
5   "Seatbelts" 2016. NHTSA

A POINT OF NONHYPOCRISY

For ten years (2007–2017), I didn't own a car; I only rode a motorcycle. I've ridden in every conceivable weather condition, including scorching 110°F plus heat, subzero temperatures, an oncoming hurricane, and a pommeling ice storm. I have flown over the handlebars, been hit by a car in a rainstorm, and laid my Harley down on the beltway around Washington, D.C. … I like to say that I have ridden straight through "ill-advised" and right into "stupid." But I still ride. If anything, these experiences excite me … but again, I'm terrified of bees. Go figure.

WE AREN'T BUILT FOR THIS

My fear of bees, my mom's fear of snakes, your childhood (or adulthood—no judgment) fear of the dark, all come from the same basic place: the history of thinking and your evolutionary biology are fighting … constantly.

Fear comes from a biological assessment and predilection for risk. Our bodies are physiologically programmed with defensive mechanisms: fight, flight, freeze, or in my case inappropriate jokes and comments.

When our body assesses risk, it assigns a response. Our heart races, our jaw drops, our eyes widen, our teeth clench, and the hair on the back of our neck stands up. Each is attached to a biological response in preparation or anticipation of risk (or engagement of some kind).[6]

---

6   Thierry Steimer. 2002. "The Biology of Fear- and Anxiety-Related Behaviors." Dialogues In Clinical Neuroscience 4 (3): 231

When our body first learned these responses and preparations, the problems included attacking predator, serious injury, or oncoming threat. However, now they are triggered by that guy stealing your parking spot, the toner being out on the copier AGAIN, or your order of the RARE steak medium coming out medium WELL!

WE RESPOND WRONG

Dr. Charles Austin Beard[7] (1874–1948) is a name you may not have heard. A scholar educated at Oxford who taught at Columbia, whose works and theories, albeit controversial, were required reading at many universities and included in textbooks on history, economics, and political science, fell from popularity in the mid-twentieth century.

On top of being a famed intellectual and academic, Beard was considered a leader of the early Progressive movement and one of the fathers of American Liberalism.

His most noted work, The Economic Interpretation of the Constitution of the United States[8] (1913), made the bold and wildly unpopular assertion that the US Founding Fathers were not the pillars of moral fiber they were (are) often heralded as, but in fact equally motivated by economic, personal financial, and semi-less honorable intentions. [9]

---

7   "Charles A. Beard Biography | AHA." 2020. Historians.Org.

8   Charles Beard, "The Economic Interpretation of the Constitution of the United States," 1913

9   Richard Drake, "Charles Austin Beard: The Return of the Master Historian of American Imperialism." Cornell University Press. Retrieved August 9, 2019

These ideas inflamed many prominent people of the time, including the president of Columbia University, his boss.

People reacted quite negatively to what they saw as an attack on the celebritized and enigmatic forefathers, who, tradition held, descended from the mountaintop with the Constitution written on stone tablets by the finger of the Almighty.

Truth be told, I might be conflating two different stories here, but fact remains people reacted poorly to Beard's claim.

Despite what many viewed as an attack or unfavorable view of the Founding Fathers, Beard commented:

"It is sobering to reflect that one of the best ways to get yourself a reputation as a dangerous citizen these days is to go about repeating the very phrases which our founding fathers used in the struggle for independence."[10]

—DR. CHARLES AUSTIN BEARD

When Columbia University, his alma mater and employer, required all its student body, faculty, and staff to take a loyalty oath to the United States in 1917, the school fired several refusing professors. Beard resigned in protest.

You may have never heard of Dr. Charles Austin Beard, his forty-seven published books, or 150 other scholarly articles

---

10 I found this quote readily available from a myriad of secondhand sources. None that I would deem scholarly nor 100 percent credible.

and papers. His contributions, albeit undeniably significant, seem to be muted.

The New School is, to this day, known for its new approaches, creative student body and faculty, and somewhat unconventional approaches and history.

Beard wanted a place where knowledge could be pursued without forced alignment or agenda, and facts and opinions could be taught, understood, categorized, and viewed as fact or opinion.[11]

Beard pushed against the rigidity of the scientific approach, and people trying to apply a scientific trial and error to historical perspectives. He yielded more to the belief in a subjective view to help guide the future. In his address as the president of the American Historical Association titled "Written History as an Act of Faith," he asserted:

"Has it not been said for a century or more that each historian who writes history is a product of his age, and that his work reflects the spirit of the times, of a nation, race, group, class, or section?

"Every student of history knows that his colleagues have been influenced in their selection and ordering of materials by their bias, prejudices, beliefs, affections, general upbringing, and experience, particularly social and economic.

---

11   "Which New Schooler Are You Most Like?" 2020. The New School.

"And if he has a sense of propriety, to say nothing of humor, he applies the canon to himself, leaving no exceptions to the rules.

"The pallor of waning of time, if not of death, rests upon the latest volume of history, fresh form the roaring press."[12]

I don't agree with everything written or reported to be said by Charles Austin Beard, but quotes like this make me think we'd have been friends. He and I both seem to have a love of history, but an equal disbelief that any real "history of thinking" could ever be possible.

We just don't have a way to accurately track thought development. We look at cultures, societies, technologies, economies, and sophisticated architectural advancements to infer the overall baseline of what a society was capable of. However, that approach is vastly short-sighted and incomplete.

People don't write down every good idea they have. We don't share every good idea we have. Many, if not most, of the ideas we do share are disregarded or misunderstood.

As members of society, we want to stick with society—we like the warmth and safety of it—which means rolling with society … even if you have a better idea. Even if you think your society is wrong, silly, backwards, or lame … where are you going to go?

---

12 Charles A. Beard, Written History as an Act of Faith -- 1933

These days we look at nonconformity with a bit of an eye roll. The label is most often applied to some eccentric individual in a cry-for-help attempt at attention, by dressing or behaving in ways counter to the norm.

Undoubtably, you went to high school with a group of teenagers who all dressed semi-identically in some clique, form, or fashion: goth, punk, emo, glam, vamp, hipsters, burnouts, freaks, geeks, comic book nerds, etc.

Invariably, these groups of "nonconformists" felt the comfort of "the pack" while straying from "the bigger pack" and often brandishing the term "nonconformist" as a semi-ironic badge of honor.

Civil disobedience is the more actionable sibling of "nonconformity." It has tended to rile people up past an eye roll. In fact, this truer form of nonconformity has led to the near deification and ultimate deaths of some of the most noted people in history. Because historically, nonconformity wasn't quite as "safe" as it is today.

In fact, when you factor in all the forms this response has taken, from simple one-off bullying all the way through genocides, ethnic cleansing, political oppression, slavery in all its forms, and more, I can argue fairly safely that nonconformity—even over cancer, heart disease, or the plague—is the riskiest, most deadly thing in history.

Throughout nearly the entirety of the past, the safest place you could be was nameless, faceless, and unimportant in the middle of the dominant pack—congratulations, Average Joe, you are historically the winner, not important enough, dangerous enough, or useful enough to be bothered with.

LIFE IS A RISKY BUSINESS

"It was great the way her mind worked. No guilt, no doubts, no fear. None of my specialties. Just the shameless pursuit of immediate gratification. What a capitalist."

—TOM CRUISE AS JOEL GOODSON, RISKY BUSINESS (1983)

What, then, do you do when you disagree with the pack? Have a better idea than the pack? Want to influence the pack, but lack the rank to appropriately do so? What if you think the pack is unanimously doing something wrong? Do you keep your mouth shut and show deference to the inherent wisdom of the masses? Or do you stand out from the crowd, take the risk?

Risk is a part of life. Every new thing we do has inherent risks, and everything we don't do has inherent risks. Succeeding can come with its share of risk, as well as, of course, failure. Life just seems to be an amalgamation of risks. This idea isn't new. But at least we can take solace in knowing that we are safer now in every possible way than at any other point in human history.

As we briefly discussed at the beginning of the chapter, the frequency with which we gauge risk incorrectly and fear the wrong things is almost funny.

Dr. Glenn Croston, a biologist and entrepreneur in the pharmaceutical drug development space, explores this concept in his book The Real Story of Risk.[13] In his introduction, he points out an amazing question: why do we as people tend to ignore concerns like heart disease, which kills as many as one in five people, but we are terrified of sharks, which at the time of this printing are responsible for nineteen shark attacks per year and only one fatality every other year.[14]

Why am I afraid of bees?! Even though I am in no way allergic, don't think getting stung hurts that bad, and have absolutely no negative childhood bee story? It's fundamentally irrational.

"The problem is that while we are marvels of evolution, we evolved in a different world. Our human nature is not adapted for the unnatural world we now live in."

—DR. GLENN CROSTON

Our physical forms, which have developed over millennia to the trials of a semi-primal life, have only existed in an industrialized society for the last hundred years or so, and in some parts of the world far less.

The "rational" side of our brains, the neocortex, has developed most recently and is not equipped with the same deep programming that our more primal brain is running. Our

---

13   Glenn Croston, "The Real Story of Risk," Prometheus 2012
14   "Human Shark Bait." 2020. National Geographic - Videos, TV Shows & Photos - Canada

"lizard brain" (the amygdala in the limbic system[15]), as it is sometimes called, affects us deeply, even when our higher self knows a situation poses no real risk.

What I found the most interesting is remarkably obvious, when you think about it:

Humans, by their own merits, have no business being at the top of the food chain.

"Humans are not the fastest animal," Croston mused. "We're not the fiercest animal, we don't have crazy fangs and claws, or armor, we're actually rather vulnerable. But what we did have going for us was that we had a social group and the ability to learn and work together."

The strength in humanity and the success of the Homo sapiens, in a vast oversimplification, were largely due to a single factor: we reason, formulate, strategize, and work as a unit. As a species, we've never been the most savage beast, but we have always been the most tactical.

But what happens when you lose that advantage? What happens when one day you are hunter three of seven in the mastodon party, but due to tribal noncompliance or overindulgence of the jellyfish salad at the tribal potluck last week, you find yourself on the tundra alone?

---

15 Joseph Troncale, "Your Lizard Brain," Psychology Today (2014)

"We are group animals that work together and if you lost that, if you were cast out on your own, you probably died," theorized Croston.

But this impulse didn't go away when we emerged from the caves. It didn't end when we moved into cities and became "civilized." A common punishment in many cultures, such as Ancient Greece and Shakespeare's Verona, was banishment.

Historically, standing out, even in a benign or positive manner, was dangerous or even fatal.

Atypical craftspeople might find themselves starving and without a way to support themselves, useless to the group. Inversely, a woman with a propensity for understanding basic herbology, chemistry, botany, or … anything, really, found herself burned at the stake. Historically: standing out = dead.

Realizing you didn't agree or understand the rules, beliefs, or customs of your society was a pretty dangerous reality. Speaking up and saying so publicly, or sometimes even privately, have also often proven fatal.

"According to most studies, people's number one fear is public speaking. Number two is death. … That means to the average person, if you go to a funeral, you're better off in the casket than doing the eulogy.

—JERRY SEINFELD[16]

---

16   Jerry Seinfeld, "I'm Telling You for the Last Time," 1998

I'm not sure of the accuracy of Mr. Seinfeld's "most" claim, but if you Google "fear of public speaking," the first several pages will extol reports and statistics repeatedly and invariably explaining that public speaking is, according to some studies, more feared than death.

What this result seems to imply is that people are in fact pretty afraid of having their knowledge, opinions, or perspective singled out.

BUT WHY?

Speaking in public is mechanically no different than speaking in private. Speaking to a few friends bears no significant difference to giving a worldwide address by satellite. Why do people who ham-it-up for their social circle become frozen by fear of speaking when in front of a crowd?

Well, the answer is actually pretty simple: they aren't.

HIPPOPOTOMONSTROSESQUIPPEDALIOPHOBIA[17]

NOUN: THE IRRATIONAL AND MORBID

FEAR OF LARGE WORDS.

(TRUTH: NOT A REAL THING.)

---

17   Annamarya Scaccia "What is Hippopotomonstrosesquippedaliophobia," Healthline, 2017, accessed Jan 10, 2020

Glossophobia[18] is the real word for "fear of speaking in public," but if you look at it from an evolutionary standpoint, the phobia has very little to do with speaking, or the public. Actually, it describes the fear of standing out. It's a fear of looking foolish. A fear of ridicule. A fear of disassociation from the group.

Glossophobia, which is merely associated with public speaking, could actually be defined as: "A primal fear the tribe won't like your story and will send you from the campfire into the cold away from the safety of the circle, to be bitten by a snake, or swarmed by lots and lots of crazy savage bees with huge stingers—like, seriously,

REALLY HUGE BEES.

But "fear of public speaking" just rolls off the tongue easier.

Another way to think about it: in the animal kingdom, being singled out rarely means something good. It tends to imply you are the strongest, and therefore a threat, or the weakest, and therefore a target. The safety of the pack exists in anonymity.

Those tend to be the natural order choices. Champion to overthrow, anonymous follower, or weak victim. Which do you want to be?

---

18   Rachel Black, "Glossophobia (Fear of Public Speaking): Are You Glossophobic?" PsyCom, accessed Jan 11, 2020

That fear of the natural order creates that deep aversion to standing out. The dread of appearing to be the target in the group is what makes our palms sweat and our heart race when we're asked to stand in front of a classroom or auditorium filled with attuned listeners. Our "lizard brain" is poised for fight or flight.

But even though "banishment" isn't really a common Western punishment anymore and social "shunning" no longer means "certain death," our bodies don't know that. Our culture, our industrialized society, and modern conveniences have created a new world over a few short generations, but our bodies are still running the evolutionary firmware of our tribal ancestors. Physiologically speaking, facing your fellows, singled out is no different than standing before the firing squad.

UNFOLLOWED, UNFRIENDED, UNFAIR

The American Historical Association states Dr. Charles Austin Beard "was one of the most daring and innovative historians of his day."[19] His ideas were unprecedented, somewhat unpopular, and received with significant derision by many of his colleagues and peers. His seminal work was in 1913, after which the vast majority of his career followed.[20]

His wife, Mary Ritter Beard, was a historian in her own right, as well as a loud and prominent suffragette. Together they

---

19 "Charles A. Beard Biography," American Historical Association, 2020, Accessed Jan 19, 2020

20 Clyde W. Barrow. *More than a historian: the political and economic thought of Charles A. Beard*," Transaction Publishers, 2000.

cowrote seven books and were at no shortage of influence and consequence in the community at the time. But as the First World War became the Second, and ultimately the Cold War, his views, his resounding isolationism, and his perceived unsavory opinions of the Founding Fathers and the Constitution were unpopular alignments, and his name and works faded from the forefront where they had been.

Dr. Charles Austin Beard stood out: he had strong, controversial, and unpopular opinions. He found success in his time, had a family, a long and prominent career, and died within society at the age of seventy-three (pretty old for 1948).

Despite his theories falling out of favor, and many being deemed "decisively refuted,"[21] you would find it hard to argue that his "bad ideas" weren't still a substantial pillar to progressing the study of US history and contributing to the society we live in today.[22]

Were his ideas wrong?
Depends on who you ask; I don't know.

Does it really matter if they were?
The answer depends on how you gauge success, I suppose.

Are his histories and insights still used and debated?
Yes.

---

21   Ellen Nore, Charles A. Beard: An Intellectual Biography (1983)
22   Peter Novick, That Noble Dream (1988) p 336.

Did his works and thoughts contribute to society?
Absolutely.

HEY, LIZARD, I'M TIRED, WOULD YOU DRIVE?

In the past, having crazy ideas was potentially fatal.

Today, it gets you an insane Instagram following.

For our forefathers, decades of experience, community compliance, and support, as well as a fair amount of luck, were the recipe for success. But our society gives billions of dollars to preening teenage Canadians with a semi-decent singing voice and the courage to put themselves out there.

History isn't just written by the winner. It is also rewritten by the second winner who beat the first winner. Then it's revised by the ancestors of the loser. Then it's collated and taught by the academic with a personal opinion, bias, and perspective.

A proper understanding of history is an essential, noble, and righteous pursuit.

But knowledge sifted through individual experience gives us each an individual perspective, which leaves us to sift through a world of data and social input and context. We have to navigate careers, families, friends, and ambitions, doing our utmost to act rationally with only partial and inherently flawed information—and often a lizard at the wheel.

CHAPTER TWO

CHANGE YOUR MIND

———

TL;DR—Innovation at its core is not building a new gadget but changing the way we think about a problem. The "Great Thinkers" in history are not people who invented new things, or designed big things, but people who reframed thought: e.g., Socrates, Plato, Aristotle.

"Think tank" is a funny term. It's an awesome concept and in practice seems like it should be the absolute perfect place to work.

If you are unfamiliar with the term or practice, a think tank is a group of people who've been deemed experts in their fields. The group works together in a combined effort to solve any number of specified problems, typically in fields of economics, politics, or development planning.

It's an attempt to fill a room with brilliance and see what brilliance emerges.

If the "infinite monkey theorem" is true (*an infinite number of monkeys at an infinite number of typewriters typing randomly will eventually recreate any given work—Shakespeare, Dickens, Austen, Dostoevsky, etc.*), then surely replacing "infinite monkeys" with "a bunch of educated people" will see true exponential results: that is, brilliance in, brilliance out.

Some truly influential and amazing think tanks are out there doing solid work. However, the often-unforeseen outcome is the promotion of group think.

For those unfamiliar with the term "group think," the *Reader's Digest* version is this: a group of people all working on the same problem together tends to discourage creativity and has a habit of just recreating the problem.

An idea is sent out into the room. It is batted around, shot down, limited with the pesky perspectives of individuals' "reality," and all that emerges is a different version of the same problem.

What think tanks need to ultimately be successful is an open forum for off-the-wall ideas, a quorum of academics willing to put their own realities in check, and a hierarchy of the great thinkers willing to apply their brilliance to other's ideas as passionately as their own.

A think tank needs people who aren't academics, per se, nor scholars with an expertise in answers; it actually needs great thinkers who aren't uncomfortable asking more questions.

Linda Emery: "A philosophy major? Now, what can you do with a philosophy major?"
Bruce Lee: "You can think deep thoughts about being unemployed."

—DRAGON: THE BRUCE LEE STORY (1994)

I CONDUCTED AN EXPERIMENT

I approached dozens of colleagues, friends, family members, and even a few bewildered individuals out on the street to ask them to name every "great thinker" they could. I got a bevy of names. The vast variety of people who made the list after only that prompt was actually remarkable.

The names (non-comprehensively, and in semi-alphabetical order) included:

Aristotle
Archimedes
Thomas Aquinas
Francis Bacon
Confucius
Noam Chomsky
Dante
Charles Dodgson
Epicurus
Euclid

Immanuel Kant
Soren Kierkegaard
Thomas Kuhn
John Locke
Niccolò Machiavelli
Friedrich Nietzsche
Plato
Ayn Rand
Sun Tsu
Socrates
Voltaire
... and, from one particularly droopy-eyed fellow,
Bob Marley.

The list was remarkably diverse. Its members span almost three THOUSAND years of history and cover a vast spectrum of fields of study and areas of interest.

However, as the questioning of my small puddle of participants continued, a few trends emerged.

First: Over 95 percent of respondents included Aristotle, Socrates, and Plato on their list.

Second: Zero percent could accurately describe in any substantive detail what those three men in particular had done to warrant being mentioned.

IN FACT: Most respondents couldn't describe any specific or definitive accomplishment or contribution of anyone on their list ... despite being ON THEIR LIST. [23]

I found this phenomenon genuinely fascinating. Apart from "God is Dead," no one knew anything about Nietzsche (seriously, NOTHING). Sun Tsu was most commonly referred to as "that war guy." Confucius, Kant, and Kierkegaard usually elicited a slew of partial or run-on sentences including fragments of dissociated details about each (seriously, I [heart] Huckabees too).[24]

Ayn Rand had the most notoriety, with people being able to name at least one of her books, although they typically admitted to never having read it. Often, they were vaguely aware of her political affiliation and country of origin ... but not many were able to follow that up with any distinct statements, actions, or strong opinions she is known to have said or carried out.

---

23 Notable exceptions:
—The gentleman who knew that Charles Dodgson was Lewis Carroll's real name was quite informed and passionate about the mathematician-turned-author, and his fair inclusion in this quorum of noted IQs.
—Likewise, those who included Noam Chomsky had a little bit more to say about his contemporary contributions to linguistics and thought.
—And the individual who included Bob Marley would be incensed if he believed I was casting aspersions on his near-encyclopedic knowledge of the musician whose contributions he purported ranked among the "biblical level."

24 I Heart Huckabees was a 2004 comedy about existentialism.

I really could go through the whole list, but they are all the same.

Some association or reference to a piece of contemporary pop culture. Sometimes a passing familiarization with a general era or piece of writing … but at the end of the day, even the individuals who could draw these names from the ether couldn't tell me why.

My semi-informal poll exceeded a hundred people (103). The entire sample group was twenty or more years old—not for any particular reason; twenty was just the youngest person I happened upon. A vast majority had a college degree, about 30 percent had a graduate degree, and approximately 10 percent had a doctorate.

I endeavored to ask an equal number of men and women, people from private and public schools, and as best I could, people from every major region of the United States and Canada.

This spread didn't seem to matter. Nearly everyone had a list of a few "great thinkers" at the ready. Nearly everyone included Aristotle, Socrates, and Plato, and no one could accurately tell me why.

A STATEMENT OF NONHYPOCRISY

Neither could I. Before the adventure of writing this book, I will say that I had heard of 99 percent of the philosophers mentioned, but was less aware of their contributions than most people I polled. Often, I only knew what had been tangentially covered within semi-associated pop culture.

In short, I more or less had the timeless philosophers of Bill S. Preston Esq. and Theodore "Ted" Logan to thank for a bulk of my background knowledge.[25]

Why were the people on that list actually on there? Why are those the names people remembered, and why exactly couldn't they tell me why?

AND I NOTICED SOMETHING PARTICULARLY INTERESTING
Everyone on the above list added structure and development to human THOUGHT.

Every one of those individuals changed the world as we know it, or at least the world for the individuals referencing them, and they did so with ONLY new perspectives, new wisdom, essentially new ways of thinking.

They weren't "inventors;" they didn't build a better mousetrap or reinvent the wheel. They looked at problems in a new way.

Archimedes "invented" the lever and the concept of pulleys and the center of gravity, and Euclid "invented" geometry. But

---

25 Bill Preston and Ted Logan, more colloquially known as Bill and Ted, had their collective works recorded in a documentary now known as Bill and Ted's Excellent Adventure and subsequently the follow-up opus, Bill and Ted's Bogus Journey. Their mantra "Be Excellent to Each Other" shaped society as we know it and gave them the label of the "Great Ones" ... if you still don't get this joke, I'm sorry ... watch more movies.

the actual contribution wasn't using a stick to move a rock, nor the number of degrees in a circle. No, their contributions were adding new ways to look at space, shapes, and logic.

The others on the list did the same, but for politics, religion, morality, and education.

What they invented were processes of thought.

They changed the world by giving us a framework. Their impacts ripple through time for little more than adding structure and shape to something undefined before it.

SOCRATES, PLATO, AND ARISTOTLE

Vizzini: I can't compete with you physically, and you're no match for my brains.
Westley: You're that smart?
Vizzini: Let me put it this way. Have you ever heard of Plato, Aristotle, Socrates?
Westley: Yes.
Vizzini: Morons.

—THE PRINCESS BRIDE (1986)

These men were mentioned more than any other individual, they were nearly always mentioned together, and they were the only recognizable group.

I wanted to know more about the people deemed great thinkers, but specifically I needed to know more about what seemed to be the second-most lauded trinity in Western culture.

These three Greek philosophers, even by individuals who cited them together, could not always be placed as contemporaries in either their time or location, of which they were both. No one could provide even a first-paragraph-on-Wikipedia-level description of their contributions. Deeper research would show that those who did confidently (or otherwise) provide any answer to the greatness of these Greeks were proven either fundamentally incorrect or so broad as to not be helpful.

But who were they? Why of the world of academics, why in the history of invention, why with a world of real-life and fictional brainiacs, are those the three who often spring to mind?

All of these men did a great number of things. College courses, doctoral dissertations, and tomes of books have been written about their collective and individual works. I, with no background in philosophy, make no attempt to do justice to their legacy.

I do not intend to explain nor add value to their narratives. What I do want to do is show what all three men had in common, apart from time and relative space; these three men followed by the rest of the aforementioned list, as well as countless others, had one remarkably important thing connecting them:

Nonconformity of Thought: A Fresh Perspective

In Reverse Chronological Order

ARISTOTLE (384–322 BCE)[26]

The student of Plato is most known for his work in developing, codifying, and defining logic and reasoning. He is responsible for dividing the schools of thought into their perspective categories: logic, metaphysics, mathematics, physics, biology, botany, politics, agriculture, medicine, dance, and theater. But even greater than that, as was explained through countless conversations with professors and students of philosophy around the country, he was the first person to truly show interest in many new fields.

He gathered the pieces, the fragments, the knowledge of others and combined them to a single voice. I'm not one for linear thinking, so come back and read this chapter again after part three, which has some interesting relevance. He explored new questions that hadn't been addressed. He posed queries and developed logical ways to address them. He touched every field of knowledge at the time. He brought them together.

He didn't just "think outside the box"; he first drew the boxes, logged and catalogued them, made new boxes that no one had thought of before, then … and only then … did he strive to think outside of them.

"The safest general characterization of the European philosophical tradition is that it consists of a series of footnotes to Plato."[27]

—ALFRED NORTH WHITEHEAD

---

26 Christopher Shields, "Aristotle," *The Stanford Encyclopedia of Philosophy* (Winter 2016 Edition), Edward N. Zalta (ed.).

27 "A.N Whitehead on Plato," The Core Curriculum, Columbia College, Accessed Jan 22, 2020

PLATO (428/427–348/347 BCE)[28]

The Alfred North Whitehead quote above might be considered "glib," but, in fact, in many ways it's true. With deeply rooted work in metaphysics and ethics, Plato developed the philosophical vocabulary and proposed the philosophical questions, many of which we are still asking today. His work The Republic is considered by some to be the cornerstone of Western culture.

Plato's dialogs observed, gathered, and gave structure to new ways of looking at old information. He asked questions of thinkers, developed new processes and ways to think. He is not necessarily someone who thought "outside the box," but more one who asked if there really was a box at all.

SOCRATES (470–399 BCE)[29]

The original nonconformist.[30] He stands as one of the first to step out of society to ask questions that no one wanted asked. He questioned authority in ways that hadn't been done previously or as publicly. He was eventually tried, convicted, and sentenced to death for corrupting the youth and not recognizing the local gods, essentially disrupting the order of society.

---

28   Richard Kraut "Plato," The Stanford Encyclopedia of Philosophy (Fall 2017 Edition), Edward N. Zalta

29   Debra Nails, "Socrates," The Stanford Encyclopedia of Philosophy (Spring 2020 Edition), Edward N. Zalta (ed.).

30   Certainly, this isn't intended to be factually or definitively true, as I'm sure at some point before Socrates a Neanderthal named "Ghrunt" was clubbed by their tribesman for not falling in line—but my point remains.

As the often-central figure in the dialogs of his most noted student, Plato, Socrates and his "Socratic Method" gave a new process and way to approach questions. Largely, it was a new way to think.

Socrates claimed he was ignorant and said he never taught anyone; he never saw himself as an intellectual or a teacher.

But for all major accounts, he was Plato's teacher, who in turn was the teacher of Aristotle. So, to put it in terms that can be more readily understood: just as Yoda to Obi Wan to Luke, Socrates stands as the philosopher who ultimately gave shape to it all.

DON'T GOOGLE IT ...

Please tell me the architect for the Great Pyramid of Giza.

Can you?

How about the emperor who commissioned the Great Wall of China?

You know that one?

If you do, what was the name of the architect?

Who engineered the aqueducts of Rome?

Do you know the genius who figured out the waterwheel mill? Or windmill?

What is the name of the programmer who created the first Graphical User Interface, permanently changing computer interactions?

If you knew the answer to those questions, that's incredible. I asked these and many others to my sample group. You would be the only one who got ANY of them.

I asked dozens of people to tell me about paradigm shifters, thought leaders, and philosophers. As illustrated above, I received a long list of names, but not one person could give me adequate reason as to why nearly any of them were important, just that they knew they were.

They didn't invent anything. They didn't create a wall or a pyramid. They didn't carve a sculpture or provide engineering significance. What did they provide? New structure to thought. They focused on new questions. What started in many respects with these three men has continued through history.

"The only true currency in this bankrupt world is what you share with someone else when you're uncool."

—PHILLIP SEYMOUR HOFFMAN AS LESTER BANGS,

ALMOST FAMOUS (2000)

– OR –

"And you can tell Rolling Stone magazine that my last words were … 'I'm on drugs!'"

BILLY CRUDUP AS RUSSELL HAMMOND,
ALMOST FAMOUS (2000)

The people we remember aren't ones who built a bigger thing, a smaller thing, a faster thing, or a slower thing. We don't actually 100 percent know the architects, craftsmen, or creators of the great pyramids in Egypt (not to say theories haven't been proposed, but they aren't names people outside of Egyptology know). For that matter, the ways and inventions of the Aztecs, who had a sophisticated society (on this continent, in relatively modern era), are also a mystery to the public at large.

But three Greeks 2,000 years ago—top of mind.

The people we remember, even if we don't know why we remember them, are the people who were more concerned at asking a different question.

The people who stand out in history, from Socrates to Stephen Hawking, are those who reframed our thinking. And, in my opinion, most importantly they did so almost 100 percent of the time alone, outside the safety of the group and often with significant opposition.

FROM THE CHEAP SEATS.
Billions of dollars each year is spent on think tanks. Even more is spent on public institutions attempting progress and

development. People are paid salaries to sit in government offices, where their entire function is to act as a roadblock, empowered and incentivized to say only "no."

We use our energy trying to buy new toys, complicated new solutions, infrastructure shifts and technological breakthroughs. Despite the fact that some of the most influential people in history, those remembered, those who changed the world, didn't build a better mousetrap. They redrew the problem.

They didn't think outside the box, they changed their mind.

CHAPTER THREE

EXTRA BACON, HOLD THE GREECE

———

TL;DR—The new ways of thinking introduced by Socrates, Plato, and Aristotle remained largely unaltered by Western society for millennia. Sir Francis Bacon and subsequently the Royal Society designed the scientific method. Sir Isaac Newton and many others were often wrong—and that's actually good news.

The iconic space shuttle we saw through a significant portion of our spacefaring history owes a portion of its proportion to that of a horse's ass.[31] Allow me to explain:

I stumbled upon this story a few years ago on the internet, which means it must be true.[32]

---

31   John Hood, "Chariots of Fire," National Review 2008, Accessed Jan 07, 2020

32   David Mikkelson, "Are U.S. Railroad Gauges Based on Roman Chariots?" Snopes 2001, accessed Jan 07, 2020

My fact-finding endeavors proved to confirm that the facts as I lay them out are genuine, but some debate is ongoing regarding whether they are coincident or causal.

Regardless, the story depicts an interesting point.

TO BOLDLY GO WHERE NO MAN HAS GONE BEFORE

Imagine, if you will, the near-iconic space shuttle in use from 1981 to 2011 sitting on the launch pad. Other than the classic black-and-white "orbiter," (which until recently I had no idea was the name of the main component), you'll remember a large red external tank and two solid rocket booster engines (SRBs) used to propel the orbiter into ... well ... orbit.

Those SRBs are the protagonist of this story. For the duration of their use they were manufactured by a Utah-based company named Thiokol. The SRBs stood taller than the orbiter—two skinny long rockets had to be that dimension as they were shipped to the launch sites by train, which lead to a bevy of logistical limitations. The train had to go through tunnels, and tunnels have very specific, fixed clearance, so the parameters were remarkably clear.

The height and width of these tunnels through the Rockies were set by the engineers of entrepreneurial visionaries J.P. Morgan and Cornelius Vanderbilt, using the best future foresight that the nineteenth century had to offer.

The breadth originally born out of the rock was sufficient to support the commerce and commute required to fit the trains of the 1800s loaded to their full capacity. That capacity was also defined by some limiting factors: namely, as heavy/high as it could for the wheelbase and clearance of the railway.

The US standard railroad gauge—or more simply put the distance between the two tracks—is four feet, eight and a half inches. That particular number is due, in large part, to the fact that the gauge is the same as that of the English tramway tracks, and many of the same engineers, builders, and fabricators of the early American railroad were British ex-Patriots.

The English tramways used that very specific number because the tram wheels were being fabricated on the same jigs as the wagons at the time, and four feet, eight and a half inches was the standard distance for wagons.

Wagon wheels used that spacing because if they didn't, they could break a wheel on longer cross country treks, as the rut in the road had been cut long before, and wagons just ran smoother if you rode them in the ruts.

By "long before," I mean literally when the roads and pathways were established during the Roman occupation of Britain. The Roman Legions made the long-distance roads to improve travel and better govern the island—and the same roads continued to be used for centuries.

The original ruts, then, were actually cut by Roman war chariots. Being military items, they all fell to a pretty specific standard, the wheel spacing by modern measurement: four feet, eight and a half inches. That size had been determined somewhat arbitrarily as the optimal width when compared and based on the size of the horses being used by the Imperial Army.

The point: The most sophisticated technology of the twentieth century was forced to account for specifications determined by an arbitrary measurement of a fallen empire, of another country, on another continent, over 1,500 years prior.

PEOPLE REALLY DON'T LIKE CHANGE

Even if not directly causal from one to the next, the fact remains that the space shuttle was limited by the tunnels and dictated by trains, and that train wheels, tram wheels, and chariot wheels were all the same width. These facts demonstrate a really long consistency.

Consistency is good. In many cases, it is safe, solid, and predictable. However, if flawed, it is problematic. If you stay the same and something else moves, it's now inaccurate. In modern science, we challenge assumptions constantly; we regroup and retest old hypotheses. Scientists can actually be fairly competitive about proving and disproving each other's theorems.

INSTAURATIO MAGNA[33]

Sir Francis Bacon is another name you may know, or one you may not. But he played a fairly significant role in making the world the one you know today. But by doing what?

Well, to vastly oversimplify: he, in his work Instauratio Magna, established the scientific method and became the father of what we now just refer to as "empirical data."

If you remember back in middle school when your science teacher explained hypothesis, theory, law concept, and the scientific method of trial and error … yes, those are all the intellectual descendants of Sir Francis Bacon. That summary might be considered a disrespectfully glib overview of the scientific method, but a complete synopsis of an earth-changing approach doesn't lend itself to brevity.

The Greeks discussed in the last chapter had, several thousand years prior, established a system to ascertain truth using assumptions. Simply put: Make an assumption, and if it tracked and proved true, it was. Then you could make new assumptions from your "proven facts."

The problem wasn't the flaws in this system, but rather to the contrary: the issue was that it worked too well, too often. It

---

33   Alban, Francis Bacon, Viscount St (1 January 1620), "Instauratio magna preliminaries," in Rees (ed.), The Oxford Francis Bacon, Vol. 11: The Instauratio magna Part II: Novum organum and Associated Texts, Oxford University Press, pp. 2–495

proved to be a system clung to and taught by scholars, academics, and students of all sorts, for millennia.

Francis Bacon was in favor of asking more questions. Challenging ideas that were only assumed with ones that could be observed. Under his system of empirical data, if information doesn't come from innate observation or experience, it doesn't count. Traditional, anecdotal, or secondhand accounts were disregarded, and only that which could be verified would be treated as fact.

This form of skepticism seems fairly obvious to us. Every parent has had the near-infuriating experience of a toddler asking "why" 347 times in a row. Complete skepticism, curiosity, question everything ... seems to be a trait we're born with.[34]

But Sir Francis Bacon was breaking with the thinking of the day, which had borderline heretical implications. His method was a breaking with all institutional knowledge and fact, challenging not just the universities, but the church and government as well. Somewhat ironically, this exact behavior led to the execution of Socrates two thousand years earlier.

Socrates and Bacon both questioned the "local gods." They both defied institutional knowledge. Socratic thought led to a system that helped define and guide understood wisdom. It was that exact system that Bacon wanted to break from.

---

34 This raises some questions for me. Did toddlers in the dark ages really not ask questions? Did they accept "because I said so"? Is there a trick to parenting that I'm missing?

Everything Right Is Wrong Again

THEY MIGHT BE GIANTS, THE PINK ALBUM 1986

Socrates, Plato, and Aristotle didn't set out to strictly define the universe and set concrete dogmas. But Socrates, with what we'd later call the "Socratic Method," established ways of asking questions and methods of categorizing or arriving at various answers.

Had Bacon been alive in their time, he'd have most likely been one of them.

Bacon was not an outward antagonist to the classic thought leadership, only the millennia of faulty assumptions and fear of breaking from established norms that followed. The scientific method and empiricism were new ways of thinking. Where Socrates established a system of asking questions, Bacon established a system of acceptable answers.

Empirical thought was a new way of processing information. Bacon didn't see the world like everybody else. Or, more fairly put, he was willing to be far more vocal about his worldview. His main work, Instauratio Magna, translates to "The Great Instauration," or "The Great Renewal," or regrowing.

Bacon wanted to trim the fat (I deeply apologize, but that absolutely needed to be said).

Bacon wanted to remove the flawed conclusions that had come from millennia of faulty assumptions. He wanted to

EXTRA BACON, HOLD THE GREECE · 69

establish schools of thought based on incontestable, natural, observable fact. His works laid the groundwork for the renowned Royal Society.

THE ROYAL SOCIETY

Or, as it was originally known: The President, Council and Fellows of the Royal Society of London for Improving Natural Knowledge.[35]

It is the oldest scientific organization in the world. Its continued impact on the world is incredible; its alumni are as noted as human minds can be and include Isaac Newton, Charles Darwin, Albert Einstein, Winston Churchill, Alan Turing, Stephen Hawking, and honorarily Elon Musk.

All names on that list, if you know them, are most likely because of their well-known aversion to the norm and way of approaching their respective fields with unprecedented perspective: gravity, evolution, relativity, unflappable diplomacy, computers, and the theory of everything.

Since 1900, the Royal Society has 280 Nobel Laureates and approximately 1,700 active members, with over 8,000 in its combined history.[36] If this section proves of particular interest for you, I recommend The Clockwork Universe: Isaac New-

---

35 "The Formal Title as Adopted in the Royal Charter" 1663 royalsociety. org, Accessed Jan 03, 2020
36 "Fellows Directory - Royal Society." Royalsociety.org. Retrieved 1 June 2019.

ton, the Royal Society, and the Birth of the Modern World by Edward Dolnick.[37]

A near infinite amount of stories can be told about the Royal Society, but simply put: it was the first, in many ways only, and definitely the longest-running organization of people whose sole motivation was to challenge assumptions, look at problems differently, cut through restrictions, and produce pure understanding.

The Royal Society looked for the perfection of complete understanding. Total skepticism.

Question everything: I've never been into the hard sciences, but the institutionalization of asking questions and challenging authority is a movement I can get behind.

SIR ISAAC NEWTON

A president of the Royal Society and the second scientist in British history to be knighted, behind only Sir Francis Bacon,[38] Newton was a nonconformist in nearly every sense of the word.

His contributions to the Royal Society being many, he is one of the two (hotly debated) fathers of modern calculus, the

---

37 Edward Dolnick, The Clockwork Universe: Isaac Newton, Royal Society, and the Birth of the Modern World, Harper Collins 2011

38 "This Day in History: Isaac Newton is Knighted." History Channel. A&E Television Networks. 20 June 2016. Retrieved August 23, 2020.

other being Gottfried Wilhelm Leibniz (#TeamLeibniz). He codified our understanding of gravity and was the first to mathematically ascertain its speed. His scientific contributions are noted and undeniable, but his brilliance in science was not what made him so remarkable.

Like those above, Sir Isaac Newton kept asking questions. He challenged authority, disregarded assumptions, redefined schools of thought, and even wrote extensively challenging the common view of the trinity and nature of God (not scientific but heretical, and potentially fatal). Newton is given his due in the ways of scientific accomplishment.

But think of it this way. Since long before we emerged from the caves, man has understood something: If you drop something, it will fall. If you trip, you will fall. If you throw it, it will eventually fall. What goes up WILL come down. These ideas were common and understood, and even in the very simplest of animals we can observe an understanding of this principle. Isaac Newton lived in the 1600s. Our recorded history goes back, as we've already discussed, thousands of years prior (give or take a few millennia).

Aristotle had delved into some of these questions and developed what is referred to as Aristotelian physics. However, it operated under a very different system in which concepts like force, mass, gravity, etc. didn't particularly make sense. They were the products of a remarkably different worldview, a different knowledge base, from a vastly different perspective.

Newton was the first person to drop an item and count to see how long it took to hit the ground.[39] His contributions were groundbreaking, but what is so striking are the facts of Newton's life that are absolutely not discussed.

Isaac Newton, as we think of him today, is a physicist. He recorded and attempted to understand everything about the nature of the physical world. However, another word that would have absolutely defined him during his life was "alchemist." Newton wrote extensively on alchemy for a significant portion of his career and on his attempt to discover the "Philosopher's Stone."

Now, those unfamiliar with Renaissance alchemy, or for that matter J.K. Rowling's books, the Philosopher's Stone was an item said to be able to turn base metals, such as lead, into precious metals, such as silver and gold. Some alchemists believed that it was also capable of producing an elixir of life.

Newton, a forefather of modern physics.

Isaac Newton, whose name stands with Archimedes, Einstein, and Hawking.

Sir Isaac Newton, the man selected to be president of the Royal Society!

---

39 Hobie Thompson and Sarah Havern, "The History of Gravity" Stanford.edu, retrieved Jan 21, 2020

THAT VERY SAME Newton spent a considerable part of his illustrious career chasing after the alchemic equivalent of King Midas' touch and the fountain of youth.

Michael Greshko, a science writer for National Geographic, wrote an article published April 4, 2016, when Newton's own recipe for Sophick Mercury (said to be the active ingredient in The Philosophers Stone) was found and released. Greshko's article included this passage:

"Newton wrote more than one million words about alchemy throughout his life, in the hope of using ancient knowledge to better explain the nature of matter—and possibly strike it rich. But academics have long tiptoed around this connection, since alchemy is usually dismissed as mystical pseudoscience full of fanciful, discredited processes.

"Newton's 1855 biographer questioned 'how a mind of such power' could take seriously 'the obvious production of a fool and a knave.'[40] And the Sophick Mercury recipe is only now resurfacing in part because Cambridge University, Newton's alma mater, turned down the opportunity to archive his alchemy recipes in 1888. The texts were sold at auction in 1936 for a combined total of just over 9,000 British pounds. Many ended up in private hands and out of scholarly reach."

Newton was fascinated by alchemy. He studied it. He pursued it. You could assert it was in many ways his life's work. He was wrong, and it isn't a big deal.

---

40   "Isaac Newton's Lost Alchemy Recipe Rediscovered," National Geographic 2016, retrieved Jan 7, 2020

His other contributions were significant. His work in other regards established the rules of the observable universe. The mind that saw the clockwork of creation also saw a possibility of amazing potential, which makes him far more of an academic hero, not less.

Modern audiences have disregarded or even suppressed his association with this whacky pseudoscience, and that might actually be the real tragedy.

WRONG IS GOOD

Isaac Newton was wrong: that is good news.

Pieces of Einstein's theory have been disproven[41] or refuted[42]: that is good news.

Stephen Hawking, for all of his modern celebrity and accomplishments, still has critics and contentions regarding some of his claims[43],[44]: that is good news.

Even people who we hold to some form of celebrated IQ were still just people, with a mixed bag of bad ideas.

---

41 Bill Andrews "5 Times Einstein Was Wrong," Astronomy.com, 2018 retrieved Jan 25, 2020

42 Mark Buchanan, "Why Einstein Was Wrong About Relativity." 2008, accessed Jan 10, 2020

43 Avery Thompson, "Scientists Rule Out Hawking Theory for Source of Dark Matter," Popular Mechanics, 2019

44 Rafi Letzter, "Hidden Gravitational Wave Signal Reveals That Black Holes Are 'Bald'" LiveScience, 2019

Some shine and change our process, others fall with a smirk and an eye roll, but these men put their ideas out there and put their name next to them, and that is important.

The classic philosophers changed the world by ignoring the standard protocol and not accepting "the way things work." In doing so, they ushered in a new era of thinking. Sir Francis Bacon and his intellectual progeny within the Royal Society cast off many traditions, established "truths," and skeptically questioned the world.

Thus, they ushered in the scientific method and a new era of thinking. Every thinker you can name became a thinker you can name by not just accepting the philosophies of men that came before them.

GET YOUR IDEAS OUT THERE

Science is exponential. New discoveries and paradigms chase out old discoveries and paradigms. They combine, overlap, and replace the concepts that precede them. Newton had some whacky ideas. Those whacky ideas came from the same brain that timed how long it took for things to fall; if we tossed out the good because of the bad, where would that leave us?

New discoveries and paradigms came in and questioned the sciences and findings of Aristotle. His works in biology and physics have been specifically refuted or disproven,[45] but that

---

45   Susan Meyer, "Leaders of the Scientific Revolution: Isaac Newton" p.22 Rosen Publishing Group 2018

doesn't diminish his relevance. Newton's laws being disproved in no way dilute his contributions,[46] and the things we are capable of will be just as great, if we can get over the fear of being wrong.

DEFINE "FACT"

Donney: "What the f**k is he talking about?"
Walter: "Forget it, Donney, you're out of your element."

STEVE BUSCEMI AND JOHN GOODMAN,

THE BIG LEBOWSKI (1998)

Daniel Patrick Moynihan was a New York senator, an ambassador, an economist, a diplomat, philosopher of sorts, and a true visionary. From him we get the oft-quoted phrase:

> *"Everyone is entitled to his own opinion,*
> *but not his own facts."*[47]

—DANIEL PATRICK MOYNIHAN

This statement is undeniably true and resonates with people of nearly all political affiliations and perspectives.

But here is my single request: define "fact."

---

46 Neil F Comins, "Discovering the Essential Universe" p.27 W.H. Freeman, 2012

47 Steven R. Weisman, "Daniel Patrick Moynihan: A Portrait in Letters of an American Visionary," Moynihan Estate 2010

Newton's "laws," which were a product of empirical evidence, have been largely disproven, but as "laws" were once considered facts.[48]

Things touted as "observable facts" have been "observed" to be incorrect. What we "know" one day has in many cases proven to be "what we deeply believed and thought" the next.

Anyone who has ever gone online has seen the same statistics and analytics used to "prove" contrary points. So, what are we to do? Nothing? Everything?

What would Socrates do?

What would Bacon do?

What would Newton do?

What should you do?

Theodore Roosevelt, in his autobiography, quoted a piece of what he called "homely philosophy":

""Do what you can, with what you've got, where you are."

—SQUIRE BILL WIDENER OF WIDENER'S VALLEY
(OFTEN MISATTRIBUTED TO THEODORE ROOSEVELT)[49,50]

---

48   Lisa Zyga, "What Happens When Newton's Third Law Is Broken?" Phys.Org, 2015
49   Sue Brewton, "Squire Bill Widener vs Theodore Roosevelt" 2014
50   Theodore Roosevelt, "Theodore Roosevelt: An Autobiography" p. 337 Charles Scribner's Sons, 1920

Much like the Greeks said, work under the assumptions you have. But much like Bacon asserted, make sure it's something you know for you, not because you were told. And later, when you find out the thing you know is "wrong" … make like Newton and keep trying to turn lead into gold.

Maya Angelou had her own take on the concept spoken on by Squire Bill:

"Do the best you can until you know better. Then when you know better, do better.[51]"

—MAYA ANGELOU

Everything we know now to be "right" was "wrong" until it wasn't. We have to use the information we have, because it is the information we have.

Fifteen hundred years ago everybody knew the Earth was the center of the universe. Five hundred years ago, everybody knew the Earth was flat and fifteen minutes ago, you knew that humans were alone on this planet.
Imagine what you'll know tomorrow.

—TOMMY LEE JONES AS K, MEN IN BLACK (1997)

---

51   Megan Angelo, "16 Unforgettable Thing Maya Angelou Wrote and Said" Glamour 2014

CHAPTER FOUR

EVERYTHING RIGHT IS WRONG AGAIN

———

TL;DR—A system of questions set up by the Greeks, a system of answers developed by Sir Francis Bacon, and our current education system are not teaching us to think. We don't teach how to understand the problem, or the answer, only the standardized process to get the acceptable answer. We have a STEM workforce crisis, in part as a result.

We've had many chapters on thought development. Socrates with his method and system for asking questions. Sir Francis Bacon and his progeny, the ensuing Royal Society, developed a system for acceptable answers. Each an anchor point in the development of "Western thought."

Science has moved forward at a somewhat exponential rate, each innovator and inventor starting from an altogether new height from their predecessor. The "ceiling" is raising as fast as the science can climb. However, in an attempt to standardize something that can't be standardized, human thought and education, the floor is not climbing proportionally (or at all).

Trellis is an organization in California led by Dr. Megan Taylor, with the goal of closing the rift this education dichotomy is causing. According to Trellis, 2.5 million STEM jobs are open in the United States, but we're seeing a significant waning in interest, engagement, and enrollment in STEM fields. Due to these and other factors, the National Association of Manufacturing and Deloitte project that number could be as high as 3.5 million by 2025.[52]

A technological explosion without a wave of interested or qualified people to fill the jobs and roles required to maintain it constitutes what BLS has labeled a "workforce crisis."

THAT'S A PROBLEM …
BUT DO WE REALLY RECOGNIZE WHAT THE PROBLEM IS?

Throughout my life, I've been continually assured of one thing: I don't think about things the way I'm supposed to.

This fact is never as evident as when someone attempts to teach me math:

---

52 Weiner, Ben. 2018. "Why the U.S. Has a STEM Shortage and How We Fix It (Part 1)." Recruiting News and Views @ Recruitingdaily

Absolutely Fictional Interchange:

Based on thousands of very real interchanges

Teacher: *Kirk, reread the problem!*

Me [reading]: *If Greg buys 18 baseballs with his allowance, and Bret buys 14 bats … What game are they PLAYING?!*

Teacher: *Kirk, finish reading!*

Me: *No, seriously, why on earth does Bret need 14 bats? And sure, Greg, you're going to lose a few balls, but are you using your allowance for the entire Little League?*

Teacher: *Okay, skip to the next one.*

Me [reading]: *Janet goes to the store to buy everything on her shopping list: rope $6.54, disposable drop cloth $1.15, bleach $3.75 … Someone needs to call the police.*

Teacher: *KIRK!*

Me: *No, seriously—she is preparing to hide a body! Look at her shopping list!!!*

I was never (rarely) trying to be difficult, and while most of my teachers liked me—I was typically the teacher's pet—certain subjects were nonstarters for me. They consisted of all subjects where "why" couldn't be answered.

If you couldn't explain WHY a "shortcut" worked in an equation or anchor a formula or theorem back to something solid, then it was never real for me. Biology, history, English, art, media production teachers, they could usually make that work. Math and chemistry teachers never could.

Word problems seemed an attempt to "anchor" a problem back to reality, but their effort never actually had the effect. Actually, often quite the opposite. It made me even more sure of the disconnect with the question/problem and the perceived "correct answer."

As a father, I watch the same pained faces of my children that I remember of myself and I relive the problem.

THE PROBLEM

We aren't teaching our children THE PROBLEM. We aren't even teaching them the solution. We are systemizing the process by which to arrive at the answer. That might sound like the same thing or at least related, but it is distinctly different.

Only in theater and media classes when doing a scene study or in my master's program did anyone ever give me an ambiguous situation and ask me to deconstruct it, ascertain if there was a problem, and determine what one or more available solutions might be.

That concept is not included in the standardized curriculum of any of the precollegiate institutions or instructors I talked with. In general, we don't teach our children to FIND the problem. I know I was never taught to understand or identify the problem.

I wasn't taught to suggest answers or solutions. In fact, in both school and my career I have been and seen leadership that actively discourages and penalizes people for proposing alternative solutions.

This approach is a large part of why we have to "show our work." Yes, a small part is to ensure honesty, that the work is our own. However, marking a correct answer "wrong" as it was arrived at "incorrectly" or through a perceived guess is something that happens in many different curricula and academic standards requirements.

Personal experience: Until grad school, outside of my truly subjective arts/film programs, I was only ever hammered into institutionalized processes. You will think like this. Here is the box: you will be graded by your adherence to it.

Clearly someone else has to see the problem with that!

FACTORY MODELED SCHOOLING

We have seen a lot of hubbub in the news over the last decade and the "factory modeled" school:

American schools were modeled after factories. And they treat students like widgets. As a consequence, learning is often irrelevant to young people—failing to target their interests or to recognize their unique needs.[53]

—JACK SCHNEIDER

However, that's an oversimplification if ever there was one. The situation is obviously far more nuanced than that. But as our current system stands, we don't ask our children if the mime is really trapped in a box, we tell them they are.

We don't ask them to ascertain anything about the box or determine whether the mime is in genuine distress. We just provide the formula for its surface area.

Dr. Peter Thaxter, a clinical psychologist who completed his graduate and postdoctoral training in pediatric psychology, works as a licensed school psychologist in the state of Virginia.

He works in the local school district conducting special-needs evaluations, as well as runs his own private practice. If that wasn't enough, he is also a lecturer and adjunct professor of cognitive neuroscience at the University of Mary Washington.

He clarified the evolution and development of the mind in relationship to learning, social behaviors, and of course, education.

"Until you get to [the] higher grades [and] education, much of teaching is following specific methods for solving problems. ...

---

53   Valerie Strauss, "American schools are modeled after factories and treat students like widgets. Right? Wrong." The Washington Post, 2015

It does differentiate for students who need different forms of support, and we might teach a few methods of getting the solution, but generally [we're] working to the agreed upon solution. That is the goal."

—DR. PETER THAXTER

Excusing away the problems there would be easy to do, by accepting and adhering to the obvious logic.

First, we teach to crawl,

Second, we teach to walk,

Third, we teach to run.

Fourth, we teach the running back handspring,

with a double tuck.

(I may have skipped a step.)

We need a progression there. The issue is that, in fact, we are attempting to force a logic train that works for some toward a brain that hasn't established that workflow yet. We are taking a malleable brain and placing it within a rigid structure, which actually acts in many ways in direct contrast to our goals.

I spoke with an elementary school teacher and mother of several children who also had significant observational experience in this arena. She asked not to have her quote attributed to her, but it was too good to not use at all:

"In my experience, kids don't get really afraid nor embarrassed by being 'wrong' until the second or third grade. Before that, they are naturally creative. and not getting the answer right is just another opportunity to guess. But after a few years of formalized education, with set instruction, they start to feel self-conscious about their answers."

The noted mathematician William Paul Thurston said:

"Mathematics is not about numbers, equations, computations, or algorithms: It is about understanding." [54]

—WILLIAM PAUL THURSTON

I love this quote, but mostly it makes me wish I'd been taught math by someone who agreed with Thurston's words. I know those teachers are out there—I just know I didn't have one.

SHOW YOUR WORK

"Show your work!" they'd say, and mark my correct answers down as wrong, because I got to the answer the "wrong way."

Dr. Thaxter taught me even a little bit more about how the brain reacts and develops, and how this all might play a role in who we are, and who we become:

---

54 Mariana Cook, "Mathematicians: An Outer View of the Inner World," p.76, American Mathematical Society 2018

"There's a certain level of experiential learning and our brain makes those connections neurologically.

"With anything that you learn, what we're doing is strengthening the connections of the neurons within your brain. And those connections that fire more often, those pathways that were action potentials are going down the line across all these different ways, the more times that connection gets made, the stronger and more efficient that connection becomes.

"The whole idea of 'use it or lose it' is absolutely true: if you don't practice things, it tends to become less salient, and those connections are not as strong later on."

This point is where a lot of different factors all come crashing in together. We take a young mind primed to draw connections and learn, eager to grow and develop; we encourage it from the home where it has experienced relative safety and support; and we introduce it into a very young, very tribal environment. It's the cutthroat world of macaroni art and finger painting, chocolate milk for lunch and plastic recorders in music class.

On the one hand, we establish the tribal structure our bodies are primed for. Simple games, simple interactions, small cliques, noncomplex social groups. On the other, we establish a currency system, approval of the overlords through a better understanding of the process. We reward with sticky gold stars and extra "pride bucks" to buy pencils, erasers, but most of all recognition.

We elevate those who best operate within the process, to come up with the preset solution that the tall overlords provide. If we act out, get the questions wrong, or don't play into the way this faculty/society is structured, our evolutionary bias is confirmed. No pride bucks, no pencil … and if we act out, we can be told we don't get to sit on the fun mat, or play with the giant parachute in gym.

The physiology of our brain creating pathways and the evolutionary bias of our bodies enforcing structure are reinforced by a system centered around a method of solution and NOT understanding the problem. Not working as a team. Not being skeptical of answers. Rather, earning a place in the society of the classroom by better mastering the system toward the agreed-upon answer. We don't get to learn about skepticism until they've largely beaten it out of us.

You are allowed to have an opinion.

You are allowed to not understand.

I encourage you to reinvent the wheel.

The books 1984 by George Orwell, Brave New World by Aldous Huxley, Anthem by Ayn Rand, and Fahrenheit 451 by Ray Bradbury all had their own flavors, politics, agendas, purposes, and underlying themes. However, all of them had one startling dystopian trend: control of information, and varying degrees of thought and innovation being a crime.

My problem as a child was that I believed them as they repeatedly told me my failure to understand was my fault. I didn't push until a method made sense. I didn't know until much later what the problem was. By then, I was very comfortable with the concept "I'm just bad at math."

I had tutors reemphasize and revisit the "approved" methods. I had countless afterschool hours beating me over the head with concepts that operated on a wavelength I did not. As I tried to express that, I was told that my not understanding was a failing of my effort, which it wasn't. I was told it was a failing of my comprehension skills, again, which it wasn't. As a child, my hands were tied and my voice in the matter was somewhat limited. However, as an adult I quickly learned: keep asking questions until you understand. Keep pushing the envelope until it makes sense.

You are allowed to think YOUR way.

You are allowed to "get it."

CHAPTER FIVE

CREDIT MISFILED

———

TL;DR—Innovation is really hard to explain, and as such, we give people credit for things they didn't do. Many innovators who were brilliant contributors to society are remembered for things they were merely associated with, while inventors are often just forgotten.

At some point in elementary school, probably around the third grade, you did a report on a great person in history. In my experience, you had a choice on how you got to present it. It could be a poster, a PowerPoint, a book report, or my personal favorite—a diorama.

With the willing or unwilling assistance of parents or siblings, you made a mess with construction paper, yarn, glue, popsicle sticks, and a shoebox to lay out a historical scene aimed to dazzle you teachers and peers (or you threw something together the night before out of random bits from around the house, no judgment).

You read what the encyclopedia had to say on the subject as well as the book the elementary library had to offer about the accomplishment. To this day, you still remember tidbits about what they did, how they did it, and why they were important.

Just one problem.

They didn't do that. Nope. That historic icon who did that amazing thing for which they are a trope in our minds— chances are they didn't do it, or at least not the way you think they did.

You learned about them throughout your whole youth. Your teacher included them in a collage about "great people in history."

You read the book about them; they totally did that thing … except they very possibly didn't. Credit and fame are funny that way.

Peter Glaser (played by Nicholas Cage): If a literary agency makes a copy of every contract … of every single contract it makes with a client and then puts it in a file, in the appropriate file … shouldn't the copy be in that file?

Therapist: Yes, I suppose it should.
Peter Glaser: It should. Right?
Therapist: Yes.
Peter Glaser: Right? Hmm. Yep, yep, yep, yep, yep, yep.
Therapist: Unless it's somehow been misfiled.

Peter Glaser: Misfiled?
Therapist: Yes, misfiled. Sometimes somebody puts a docu-
ment in the wrong file and then it's misfiled. It makes it much
harder to find.
Peter Glaser: Who? Who? What do you mean? Who?!

THE VAMPIRE'S KISS, 1988

On the journey to better understand thought leaders, rule
breakers, and nonconformists, a pretty solid theme revealed
itself. An absurd number of times I'd start reading about
someone I'd grown up "knowing" about, or a person whose
contributions are taken for granted so much that they are
almost axioms in our dialog. Ridiculously often, I realized
these individuals absolutely deserved a place in our history
books, but very often NOT for what they are known for.

Thomas Edison is my favorite example of a person who gets
almost no credit for what he did, and copious amounts of
credit for things he didn't do.

Thomas Edison didn't personally invent a vast majority of the
patents he held. HE DID NOT invent the light bulb.[55] The
empire he built was based far more on his business position-
ing and "charm"[56] (read: New Jersey thug) than on invention,
and he muscled under and acquired far more ideas than he
personally had. He still built an empire. He was still very
much "brilliant," just not for what he is generally credited for.

---

55   Scott Berkun, "The Myths of Innovation" ch. 5, O'Reilly, 2010
56   "History of the Lightbulb" Energy.gov, retrieved Jan 25, 2020

One of my absolute heroes in the history of film is William Kennedy-Laurie Dickson. (W.K.L Dickson.) This man invented the motion picture camera, or to be most technically accurate, the kinetograph camera and kinetoscope viewer, which constituted the first commercially successful motion picture system.

The stories vary semi-wildly from source to source, depending on who commissioned the history to be told. If the Library of Congress and the Edison museum narrative are to be believed, [57] Dickson was a beloved assistant and chief associate who assembled these devices at Edison's instruction and behest. However, according to most other accounts, Dickson cobbled together the prototypes on his own time, as Edison didn't have faith or interest in the project.[58]

The undisputed part is this: WKL Dickson designed and created the first working cinema system. Designed an early prototype of "talking pictures," designed and oversaw the construction of Edison's famed studio, The Black Maria, and personally produced hundreds of films, including being the first person to film the pope (Leo XIII).

No version of the narrative doesn't have WKL Dickson as the designer, engineer, and craftsman to make movies possible. He lived to be seventy-five years old; he would see motion

---

57 "1893: Edison Records First Sneeze on Film" APS.org 2001, accessed Jan 11, 2020

58 "Thomas Edison Patented the Kinetoscope" America's Story, from America's Library, accessed Jan 20, 2020

pictures and talkies sweep the world as a sensation, but be uncompensated and uncredited until after his death in 1935. Due to conflicts with Edison, his name wasn't included in the contribution to the industry until much later.

This example is just one of many. I wasn't even looking for them and found dozens. WKL Dickson received no credit. Edison received recognition he deserved and credit he didn't. Over and over again. Edison was an innovator. He saw opportunities. Dickson was an inventor. These are very different things.

FROM MOVIES TO MOTORCARS

My SOUL is an ISLAND ... my car is a Ford.

SHE'S ALL THAT, PERFORMANCE ART SCENE, 1999

One of my all-time favorite quotes is attributed to Henry Ford of Ford Motorcars and says:

> *"If I'd asked people what they wanted,*
> *they'd have told me 'a faster horse.'"*
>
> —HENRY FORD

In my experience, this quote is used in a variety of contexts, but most often by assertive entrepreneurs disregarding audience data. I love data, truly. I use this quote all the time, because it is so useful to help pop the "audience is always right" paradigm.

I love the simplicity and resonance of this quote. I tend to modernize it to the statement: "I promise to give you what you need; I can't promise it will be what you asked for."

However, the Ford quote tends to resonate with people and the groundbreaking effect Henry Ford, his foresight, and his general "brilliance" had on the United States and American culture. Unfortunately, we can identify some glaring problems:

First, this quote very much implies that Henry Ford had something to do with the invention of the motorcar. He didn't. The first steam-powered car was produced in the 1790s,[59] and Karl Benz patented the first working combustion engine motorcar in 1885 in Germany.[60]

Not to mention that Charles and J. Frank Duryea of Wyoming produced the first gasoline-powered automobile in America in 1893, a decade before Ford motorcars opened their doors.[1]

Second, and by far most importantly, no evidence supports Henry Ford actually saying this. All references to this quote started long after his death, and even the Ford museum can't and won't confirm its authenticity.

It stands as a great attention-grabbing mantra, however, and if anything, actually does a disservice to the contributions that Ford did, in fact, make.

---

59   Nicolas-Joseph Cugnot, Brittanica.com retrieved Jan 20, 2020
60   AG Daimler, "The birth of the automobile." Archived from the original on 21 November 2015. Retrieved 1 October 2014

WHAT DID FORD DO, EXACTLY?

If you asked a hundred walk-about Americans what Ford did, a large number would tell you of his invention and innovation of the production assembly line. Which, sadly, he also, sort of, didn't do … he only motorized it.

1. James Flink, The Automobile Idea. (1990). MIT Press. p. 5.
2. "Henry Ford," Biography 2019, Accessed on Jan 11, 2020
3. "Henry Ford - Visionaries On Innovation - The Henry Ford." 2020. Thehenryford.Org.

Richard Garrett & Sons, an English producer of steam engines, incorporated a production-line workflow into what they called the Long Shop in 1853.[61]

In America, Ransom E. Olds of Oldsmobile fame patented an updated variation in 1901.[62]

Henry Ford might be one of the most classic examples of this remarkably important discrepancy in modern thinking and vernacular. Henry Ford wasn't an inventor. He didn't really invent anything. Henry Ford was an engineer, rethinker, and most importantly an innovator.

Ford is given no shortage of credit for his contributions. However, his contributions being so hard to simply qualify, he is credited for a lot he had nothing to do with.

---

61 "The Long Shop Museum » Richard Garrett and Sons." 2020. Longshopmuseum.Co.Uk.

62 Ransom E. Olds, Automotive Hall of fame 2020, Automotivehalloffame.org

The assembly line, in concept, already existed. Cars were already in mass production and for sale. Ford's contribution was far more radical. Related to Peter Drucker's quote mentioned in the Introduction, Ford used his knowledge in both doing something he knew to make it more efficient, and with things he didn't, to greatly innovate the process.

He developed systems combining data from vast areas, spanning production to business expertise to design. He incorporated knowledge from countless fields to produce cars faster, in higher volumes, at lower costs, in a form factor that appealed to a huge cross section of people.

Again, with the nonlinear thinking—read this chapter again after Part 3.

HENRY FORD USED THE CROSS SECTION OF ALL HIS EXPERIENCE TO CHANGE HOW PEOPLE THOUGHT ABOUT CARS.

Henry Ford was raised on a farm in Michigan in the 1860s and '70s. Fascinated by machines and how things worked, he studied them. He talked to the men who ran steam engines, and he took apart watches and other small objects he could get his hands on to teach himself how to fix them. He chose to forego farming with his father and went to apprentice under a manufacturer of railway cars in 1879.

Skipping a few chapters ahead, he went to work as an engineer for the Edison Illuminating Company in 1891. This tidbit is mostly interesting due to the fact that, as a farm boy who apprenticed on steam engines, he didn't know anything about electricity or electric lights. But his overall fascination with how things worked drove him to the job so he could better learn about it all up close.

By 1896, he was chief engineer of the Edison Illumination Company, but spent his nights tinkering in his garage with his friends on a "horseless carriage," which, as mentioned above, the Duryea brothers had already been using to cruise main street and impress the ladies for three years at this point.[63] But friends tinkering on assorted projects in a garage is a pastime for the ages, and that is just what Henry spent his free time doing.

Early cars were a toy for the elite. They were a relatively well-known entity, but were not accessible in price nor function for the working American. That is what Henry Ford changed. He championed cars for the middle class. A quote from the Henry Ford Museum of American Innovation describes him best:

"Henry Ford took inspiration from the past, saw opportunities for the future, and believed in technology as a force for improving people's lives.
"To him, technology wasn't just a source of profits, it was a way to harness new ideas and, ultimately, further democratize American life."
—THE HENRY FORD MUSEUM OF AMERICAN INNOVATION

---

63 I have no historical knowledge of this, and it is most likely not true ...
     unless it is ...

He was successful. In the summer of 1896, he made a working "Quadricycle," which was more or less a bathtub with wheels that steered like a boat, but it ran. In 1898, he would do it again: he and a team of four friends would create their second operational "horseless carriage," which was the proof point that Henry needed.[64]

This feat wasn't proof he was a good engineer, nor even that he could design and make a motorcar—that fact was abundantly clear already. The proof point was that he could lead a team, articulate a vision of something that had never been done, manage the project, and see it to completion. This twice repeatable fact was what he used to convince a group of businessmen to invest in him for a company to make horseless carriages.

As many engineers and would-be entrepreneurs will tell you, running a business isn't as easy as it looks and "learning by doing" involves falling down, a lot. So, he did.

His first company utterly failed. As did his second. Not until after sufficient trial and lots and lots of error did Henry Ford secure his third round of investing and incorporate the Ford Motor Company in 1903.

The failures didn't stop there. We've all heard of the Model T Ford. It was named the most influential car of the century and sold millions of units in very early US history.

---

64 "Henry Ford - Visionaries on Innovation - The Henry Ford." 2020. Thehenryford.Org.

But what isn't instantly nor inherently obvious is that his first car was the Model A, and his second car the Model B. The model T, his success, was his twentieth attempt at a car.

Of his designs and processes, he said:

"I will build a motor car for the great multitude. It will be large enough for the family, but small enough for the individual to run and care for. It will be constructed of the best materials, by the best men to be hired, after the simplest designs that modern engineering can devise.

"But it will be so low in price that no man making a good salary will be unable to own one—and enjoy with his family the blessing of hours of pleasure in God's great open spaces."[65]

And he did. But that is about his "invention." Far more important was Henry's innovation. Which, again, is harder to simply qualify. But it really boils down to this quote:

"Be ready to revise any system, scrap any method, abandon any theory, if the success of the job requires it." [66]

—HENRY FORD

---

65   "The Model T | Johns Hopkins University Press Books." 2020. Jhupbooks.Press.Jhu.Edu.

66   "How Ford Is Innovating With Materials Science." 2020. Fortune.

Henry's real success was in diversity of thought. His approach was counter to the status quo. He incorporated methods and abilities from multiple industries and a significant number of failed attempts. What Henry Ford "did" was throw out the rules of what a car "was" or how it "was" done. He took all his diverse knowledge and strained it through a new perspective.

The innovator looks past the tradition. Looks past the assumption. Looks past what he "knows to be true" to find what he "needs to succeed."

BACK TO THIRD GRADE

That person in your diorama was significant; your teacher was correct about that. They probably did change the world, but I've found it unlikely that they did the thing your teacher said they did …

See, their credit was misfiled.

CHAPTER SIX

—GLYPHS ON WALLS—

WE'VE GONE FULL CIRCLE

TL;DR—The most remembered people in history are the Conqueror and the Communicator. But successful versions of both are, in truth, innovators.

Given his impassioned face, epic hair, confidence in tone and tenor, we watchers of docutainment television[67] are forced to ask a question that goes to the very fiber of society:

Could the Aliens dude from the history channel really be "wrong"?

As we close out "The History of Thinking," I'll share my key takeaways from my time studying it: our ability to articulate

---

67 Docutainment television is a phrase I totally did not make up that describes any/all shows that are equal parts documentary and entertainment. It includes almost anything on the Discovery Channel, Science Channel, History Channel, or National Geographic.

and explain the history of human development is based off our understanding of other cultures' relationships to their media and prevalent form of communication at the time.

Then historians, anthropologists, and sociologists attempt to chronicle it, categorize it, encapsulate it, and curriculumize it. *(truth be told, not sure "curriculumize" is a real word)*

SIMPLY PUT

We can't really chronicle thought, and even chronicling society is limited to the records kept. It has been tied very much to media, its complexity, distribution, reception, and general medium. But as nearly any parent can tell you:

Take the numbers off a connect-the-dots puzzle and hand it to a room full of children, and the resulting pictures will vary wildly in complexity, completion, coherency, and creativity.

Without the context of the numbers, we are left with our assumptions of what each dot means. We are left to create a phoenix from the ashes of history, when in life the bird was really a turkey.

Cave paintings were the stories of a particular people: entertainment or recordings of events, we don't fully know.

- Did that squiggly line kill that mastodon … or ask it to dance? We can't actually be sure.

– This group of orange stick figures either really likes this group of black stick figures or are throwing spears at them … unclear.

We don't know what they were saying, and we assume. But without the accompanying story, these cave paintings do little to articulate the tale.

Egyptian hieroglyphs and papyruses have been found at everything from religions rites to pre-Kama Sutra style erotica.[68]

– "On this wall in the main hall we have a sacred rite of the family being honored by their gods."
– "This clay pot, however, seems to be the Egyptian equivalent of the homeowner's sock drawer."

Egyptologists redefine what we think we know about ancient Egypt every decade or so. Because as clearly advanced as they were, their record-keeping varied greatly in its clarity—which makes assuming/knowing much about them fairly difficult to be conclusive.

The first written words using an alphabet (we've found) were receipts, ledgers, recordings of accounting, and historical information.[69]

---

68 "How The Oldest Depiction of Sex Changed the Way We See the Ancient Egyptians." 2019. Culturacolectiva.Com.
69 "Phoenicians: Sailing Away [Ushistory.Org]." 2020. Ushistory.Org.

- So, the Phoenicians were just the world's first organization of CPAs?
- Are we really to believe there wasn't a single dime-store thriller cranked out with the shiny new alphabet?

It is actually fairly unremarkable that the brains system-based enough to alphabetize their phonics and symbolize the sounds they could make would do so out of a systemic need for better accounting. Yeah … that one tracks.

Then Gutenberg's moveable type and printing press really changed the game.

- Books, newspapers, and magazines were the standard formats of the printed word.
- Catalogs, periodicals, trade magazines, and reports were produced, along with dime novels and pulp fiction, pop art and early comics.
- The sheer abundance of media in various forms gave new and unprecedented ability to communicate new thoughts and concepts …
- Most prevailing thing printed to date? The Bible.[70]

Many modern books, papers, dissertations, documentaries, and wide-eyed theorists can take this constellation of characteristics and draw almost any conclusion about these cultures. (Aliens.) We only know what we know; we can only gather conclusions through our own perspectives.

---

70 "Best-Selling Book." 2020. Guinness World Records.

Not to get too far ahead into the book: this concept goes for your boss and coworkers too. We are "prisoners" to our time and point of view. Sharing a different drawing derived from an unnumbered connect the dots isn't "bucking the system"—it's just sharing.

But just as we learned, Cambridge suppressed Newton's work in alchemy, and you were unceremoniously shot down at that meeting and told in some way to "know your place." This common practice hardly allows us to compile a fitting timeline of how previous societies thought, what they thought, or even what they were capable of comprehending. We can't even create a definitive depiction of the people.

However, within this top-level view of world history, we find that the people who stand out fall into essentially two categories.

THE COMMUNICATOR AND THE CONQUEROR

THE COMMUNICATOR

Alexander Hamilton has been mentioned a lot over the last decade, with Lin Manuel Miranda's hit Broadway musical, which turns Hamilton's crazy life into an even more amazing, albeit semi-fictitious story. Alexander Hamilton was a communicator, which is why people knew how good he was. Benjamin Franklin and Thomas Jefferson—also both communicators. Winston Churchill, John F. Kennedy, Martin Luther King Jr., Oprah Winfrey: communicators. The people on the noncomprehensive list of philosophers and thought leaders who opened this section, even to include Bob Marley, are on there for changing the way people think, for their ability to communicate the differences.

THE CONQUEROR

However, Washington, Alexander the Great, Genghis Khan, George Patton, conquerors. Rapiers or rhetoric, how did they fight? George Washington is famed for not being power-hungry. He was a strategist, tactician, and master of espionage, but he truly just wanted to be a farmer. However, his contributions are still that of conqueror, and most of the quotes we know of him were written or delivered by his speechwriter and right-hand man, Alexander Hamilton.

But as a person who has served in the military, was raised by a career soldier, and has spent a significant portion of his life working with the armed forces, I can assure you: the "conquerors" who rise to the top are those who can adequately communicate their vision, and can both think similarly to and differently from the enemy.

BUT ARE THESE "HEADINGS" OR "SUB-HEADINGS?"

The Communicator and the Conqueror, the only two types of people who have made a significant impact on history, both find success in doing the exact same thing:

INNOVATION: Combatting perceptions and assumptions, adapting to what is right, disregarding what is wrong, and maneuvering through the change.

In this section we dove into the history and the structure of thinking. The individuals whose contributions to thought leadership played a role into our current society. We discussed some of the science of why we think the way we do and how we can overcome some of those things.

We are limited greatly by the media of cultures that none of us have firsthand memories of, and the accounts we do have are from people whose perspectives and lives were quite different than our own.

We piece together the sudoku puzzle of history, filling in the numbers by the process of elimination, creating a picture with our understanding of how the pieces "should" fit together. We do our best.

Our first recorded communication was pictographically represented stories of our perceptions of reality. Shared moments, achievements, fears, or hopes. We emerged from the caves sharing pictures on our walls. Representing our emotions with colors, shapes, and symbols.

The Egyptian hieroglyphs and the many mysteries surrounding them and the culture of who carved them is an entire field of scholastic research, and it is still—just pictures on walls. Now we stand in a modern world, I'm not quite sure that our social media is serving any different purpose, only a larger scale.

But let's not get ahead of ourselves…

CHAPTER SEVEN

COGNITION, COMMUNICATION, AND CLOSE-UPS

———

TL;DR—The drip of media and communication becomes a waterfall with modern media. The future is changing at an exponential rate. New media allows for, encourages, and creates new ways of thinking.

THE ONE-TWO-THREE PUNCH INTO MODERN MEDIA

We're missing so much, between people not writing down their "bad" ideas and authorities suppressing ideas they thought were bad, as well as the expense and time of media production and cost and effort of producing, transporting, and preserving media. Fact of the matter is, we are missing a lot of history.

That is before we start factoring in things like armies destroying the records of occupied nations, or the great fire at the Library of Alexandria.

The only sources we have to even attempt to glean an understanding of those that came before us are their records and histories, and an attempt to see things from a perspective we can't possibly hope to fully understand.

I'm a lover of history and believe everyone should endeavor to study it as it is relevant to all of us. But as Dr. Austin Charles Beard stated, engaging with history must be done with the subjective understanding of unreachable perspective.

The old media we have is invaluable; it gives us great insight into our forefathers and the decisions they made with information they had. But information in the past was inherently limited, and information FROM the past isn't much better.

Too little, too fragile, often without proper context.

But the landscape started to change dramatically in 1877:

First, Edward Muybridge developed the technique that would lead to the motion pictures: he lined cameras up and took pictures of a running horse to create a stop-motion image.[71]

---

71 Muybridge, Eadweard; Mozley, Anita Ventura (foreword) (1887). Muybridge's Complete Human and Animal Locomotion: All 781 Plates from the 1887 Animal Locomotion. Courier Dover Publications. p. xvii.

Second, Italian inventor Guglielmo Marconi proved the viability of radio communication in 1895.[72]

Finally, Philo Farnsworth invented the cathode ray tube and transmitter and created television in 1927.[73]

These three advances were entirely unrelated. But they, only approximately twenty-five years apart, each represent an entirely new form of communication. They changed the way we could tell stories, receive stories, and analyze problems. They allowed for visual and audio communication across vast distances.

COGNITION

As we will discuss at length in a future chapter, a great many scary sounding words relate to the study of the brain. Psychology, psychiatry, neurology, etc. My favorite, and by far the most important here, is: cognition.

COGNITIVE SCIENCE MERITS DEFINING (BRIEFLY)[74]

Psychology and psychiatry focus on largely "how you think" from a process standpoint, and neurology is more about the architecture and actual organ that is your brain and nervous system.[75]

---

72 BBC Wales, "Marconi's Waves." *Archived from the* original *on 20 January 2007.* Retrieved 20 January 2007

73 Schatzkin, Paul (2002), The Boy Who Invented Television. Silver Spring, Maryland: Teamcom Books, p. 50.

74 "Cognitive Science," (Stanford Encyclopedia Of Philosophy). 2020. Plato.Stanford.Edu.

75 "Cognitive Science - An Overview | Sciencedirect Topics." 2020. Sciencedirect.Com.

Cognition is the mental action or process of acquiring knowledge and understanding through thought, experience, and senses. It leads into sensation, notions, intuition, and my favorite—perceptions!

When it comes to media, this topic is relevant

In antiquity the way to learn was through experience,
                                                    if it didn't kill you.

Or through a teacher,
                                        if it didn't kill them.

Or through reading,
            a slow process that statistically you couldn't do.

This reality made new information and new processes fairly inaccessible.

But the onset of radio, motion pictures, and television opened up new ways to input, code, and process information. These new technologies changed the way we could tell and hear stories.

This innovation led to a new way of thinking. Access to information quickly, allowing new forms of cognition, reacting to new parts of the brain, allowing storytellers and news bearers to stimulate the visual and auditory cortex.

This development changed how information could be consumed.

It changed how information could be understood.

Overly simplified and inherently flawed analogy:

Media and Communication = Thought

—THEREFORE—

New Media and New Forms of Communication = New Ways to Think

Thinking is tied directly to communication. When a person develops a new concept or outlook, it is only as good as their ability to explain, convey, or articulate it.

With photographs, moving pictures, radio, and television, we had several new arrows in our human ability to tell stories, articulate problems, and convey solutions.

WITH NEW COMMUNICATIONS CAME NEW THOUGHT
Only fifty years after the television, we would start seeing early home computers. Only ten to twelve years after that, the screeching wailing of dialup internet and communications,

data, and the relationship between people and information would never be the same.

We would go from three channels on a television to near infinite. Our ability to consume media is limited only by our imagination and our internet connection speed.

This affected every possible facet of life.
Our demonstrated decision-making is different.
We communicate differently.
We research differently.

All of this is related to one near inescapable observation:

New capabilities with media and a change in how we communicate affected the very essence of how we think.

A study published in the US National Library of Medicine by lead neuroscientist Dr. HJ Kretschmann reports the human brain actually grows and develops faster than it did one hundred years ago. [76]

Another study by lead psychologist Dr. Joseph Firth on the "Online Brain"[77] explored changes in our memory, attention,

---

76   Kretschmann HJ, et al. 2020. "Human Brain Growth in the 19th and 20th Century. - PubMed - NCBI." Ncbi.Nlm.Nih.Gov.

77   Firth, Joseph, John Torous, Brendon Stubbs, Josh A. Firth, Genevieve Z. Steiner, Lee Smith, and Mario Alvarez-Jimenez et al. 2019. "The 'Online Brain': How the Internet May Be Changing Our Cognition." World Psychiatry 18

social structure, and more—all in relation to new trends in media consumption.

We are processing information that is changing at an exponential rate. For nearly 1,000 years of the Dark Ages, negligible technological or social developments emerged. Using a time machine to arrive in 500 AD versus 1500 AD would have very marginal, if any, cultural, technological, or otherwise significant changes in the way people lived.

However, using that time machine to arrive in twenty-year intervals from roughly 1860—present, massive changes have occurred, branching out over every sector of human lifestyle:[78]

- In the late 1880s, cars were an uncommon, rich-person toy.
- Manned flight was science fiction.
- Computers weren't even in science fiction of the time.
- However, not one hundred years later, in the 1980s:
- Cars were a ubiquitous standard and a major industry.
- We not only knew that manned flight was possible, but commercial airlines were booming.
- We had satellites.
- A man landed on the moon.
- A shuttle program and development of an International Space Station.
- Computers weren't a standard in homes yet, but they would be relatively soon.

---

78 "History of Technology - From the Middle Ages to 1750."
2020. Encyclopedia Britannica.

That's a lot for one hundred years. We aren't even fifty years past that point, but the change is exponential. Artificial intelligence and machine learning make up a considerable part of the production industry. Cars were already a massive industry fifty years ago. But today we produce more cars, with more features, in more variations, and employ significantly less people.

Computers are now not just in every house, but every human has between one and three personal devices with more computing power than the computer fifty years earlier that put rockets into orbit and safely landed people on the moon.

We have new communications channels, with which comes new languages, new publics, new vernaculars, new ways of processing information. Our data intake and output change almost yearly, but the physiology of our bodies is still the result of tens of thousands of years of evolution that have trained us to live in conditions that are no longer representative of our lifestyle.

Virtual reality is becoming the next hurdle. With haptic and kinetic sensors and 360-degree treadmills and immersive movies and content, we will once again have to brace ourselves for a new paradigm of processing. The History of Thinking will have a new chapter.

"Spirit!" said Scrooge in a broken voice, "remove me from this place."

"I told you these were shadows of the things that have been," said the Ghost. "That they are what they are, do not blame me!"

"Remove me!" Scrooge exclaimed, "I cannot bear it!"

He turned upon the Ghost and seeing that it looked upon him with a face, in which in some strange way there were fragments of all the faces it had shown him, wrestled with it.

"Leave me! Take me back. Haunt me no longer!"

—THE CHRISTMAS CAROL BY CHARLES DICKENS,
CONCLUSION OF STAVE 2, "THE FIRST OF THREE SPIRITS"

THE GHOSTS OF INNOVATION PAST (SORT OF)

This was never intended to be a "History Book," but as with all messages and communications, we needed to be on the same page before we go into Part 2. However, if you got anything from Part 1, I hope it was this:

History is full of forgotten people with undoubtably amazing, groundbreaking, paradigm-changing ideas that were ignored. Meanwhile, we remember people and censor their bad ideas. We forget people who were the best rule followers and elevate people who thought that the rules didn't make sense. Our brains' software updates and diverges daily, sometimes dozens of times, while the firmware of our bodies is still using an upgrade patch from roughly 7,000 years ago.

Technology changes our world, no doubt about that. But the advances that broke the mold of society were thoughts. As you read back through the world history, two things pop up.

First: Societally, culturally, anthropologically, and technologically, our lives are incomparable and exponentially different from even one generation ago, let alone hundreds of years.

Second: Biologically, we are the same species that rode the tyrannosaurus rex into battle and entered society with the help of aliens (unless the internet is wrong).

Our framework is the same as those who lived in packs and hunted, keeping each other alive as a tribe. We learned to fear the unknown as it wasn't safe, and we feared being alone, as it almost always meant death.

Our history gives us little context for the handling of modern problems, as they are done within a structure that was science fiction even within our own lifetimes. However, we are the same base animal as George Washington, Socrates, and Gilgamesh the Mesopotamian.

Real innovation isn't about adding technology, new tools, new doodads, and dingle hoppers. Our technology has already quite literally developed a mind of its own. True innovation is to add to our thoughts—develop sophisticated new processes that aren't extensions of posting our achievements on walls.

The people we remember—the conquerors, the communicators, the philosophers, and the leaders—weren't the engineers with new tech. They added new thought.

Pulitzer and Hearst, they think they got us …

Do they got us? NO!

—CHRISTIAN BALE AS JACK KELLY, NEWSIES, 1994

PART TWO

MAKE FRIENDS
WITH THE MOUSE

CHAPTER EIGHT

I'M NOT PEDANTIC, JUST OVERLY PRECISE

———

TL;DR—Words are programming. Axioms and statements like "Build a better mousetrap" actually hurt innovation, as they draw parameters and exclude potential solutions from an undefined goal. We need to be clearer and more careful in how we define goals and acceptable outcomes.

Disclaimer:
Words and clarity matter.

Second Disclaimer:
When someone disregards your objection as just being "semantics," what they are actually saying is: "I have no idea what semantics are, and no interest in any clarity you might be attempting. Please stop disagreeing with me—HEY, LOOK, A THREE SYLLABLE WORD!"

Third Disclaimer: I really don't try to be pedantic; it just comes naturally.

Throughout all of Part 2, I will cling to the wording of an axiom that was never intended to be taken literally:

"If you build a better mousetrap, the world will beat a path to your door."

—RALPH WALDO EMMERSON

I will include a great many passages to which the response could generally be "damnit, Kirk, lighten up; it was a metaphor!" and I agree with you. Every time you see one of those moments, trust me, I saw it too. So, why did I cling so myopically at the literality of a metaphor?

It's a metaphor. (Wow, this just got meta.)

We, as a culture, use words wrong. We often employ other people to be extensions of ourselves rather than whole persons of their own helping us. We ask for the wrong things, describe them the wrong way, communicate what we need somewhat incoherently and think about it all backward.

As we wrapped up Part 1 with media being equivalent to thought processes, keep in mind that words matter. I'm not saying we can't misspeak or use the wrong term. I'm not implying that true synonyms don't exist in the world. But for the most part, we have a problem asking for OUR solution, rather than a problem be fixed.

We don't allow someone to fix a problem. We instruct them to sift all the information through our own perspective and come out with the solution we would have arrived at.

This approach isn't actually possible, not to mention it's a terrible practice—demeaning, belittling, ineffective, and inefficient.

So, yes, over the next several chapters, I will cling with pedantic fervor to a metaphor, as if it is literal.

It's a metaphor; just go with it.
"Earthman, the planet you lived on was commissioned, paid for, and run by mice. It was destroyed five minutes before the completion of the purpose for which it was built, and we've got to build another one."

Only one word registered with Arthur.
"Mice?" he said.
"Indeed Earthman."
"Look, sorry—are we talking about the little white furry things with the cheese fixation and women standing on tables screaming in early sixties sitcoms?"

—DOUGLAS ADAMS, HITCHHIKER'S GUIDE TO THE GALAXY

LITERAL—LITERACY—LITERARILY

The statement few of us have actually heard reads:

"If a man has good corn or wood, or boards, or pigs, to sell, or can make better chairs or knives, crucibles or church organs, than anybody else, you will find a broad hard-beaten road to his house, though it be in the woods."[79]

—RALPH WALDO EMERSON

79 "Build a Better Mousetrap." 2011. National Museum of American History.

Somewhere along the way this statement was taken and simplified. The lilting prose of Emerson was removed, the colloquial examples shortened and softened, leaving the phrase, sometimes with its original attributions, but far more often just an anonymous axiom:

"Build a better mousetrap, and the world will beat a path to your door."

While significantly different, the spirit of both phrases is the same:

New inventions and quality products will drive the market.

People are drawn to the new, the better, the cutting edge. We can name thousands of examples: from mile-long lines outside electronics stores before the release of a new gadget, to seven-figure bounties offered for leaked information on as of yet unreleased tech. People love the new, the different, the exciting, the better… which is confusing, as we already discussed, because people don't like change.

We have heard thousands of times, "Don't reinvent the wheel," a phrase that at its core makes remarkably little sense, as the wheel has and continues to see remarkable improvements and modifications over its life span since first recorded in Mesopotamia in 3500 BCE.

Often attributed for the rise of human civilization, the invention of the wheel will be covered at length in a later chapter, but what began as a potter's spinning disk was transferred to the bottom of heavy things to help them move. Solid became spoked, materials continued to shift, tires developed, along with new sizes, shapes, grip patterns, water displacement patterns, traction, material types.

Self-inflating, solid rubber, standard four wheels, two wheels, six wheels, eighteen wheels. Slick tires, off-road tires, snow tires, inner-tube tires, radial tires, optimized for all-wheel drive, four-wheel drive, rear wheel drive. Trains used fixed axels on tracks; tanks and other all-terrain vehicles use a series of wheels powering a single interconnected track and tread.

The wheel has been nearly continually reinvented. I see no evidence that reality is going to change anytime soon, as GM has recently announced its next iteration, the airless tire, will be on its vehicles by 2024, while Continental has gone the exact opposite direction, and its tires will soon be self-inflating. I don't want to spoil the upcoming chapter on this very subject, so let's get back on topic.

"Reinventing the wheel" is a positive thing; once we've stopped questioning, we stop progressing.

As a counterpoint to an axiom about not reinventing something that has been near constantly reinvented, the Emerson axiom has an equally formidable "problem." The "Build a better mousetrap" statement is a puzzle taken on by many. Mousetraps exist in near every form; not only does the expression stand as somewhat of a general challenge, but it has become shorthand for "fix the unfixable problem."

The problem with this problem is that it prescribes a solution without addressing the problem itself.

- Do you want to capture the mouse?

- Kill the mouse?

- Prevent the mouse from coming in?

- Do you want to bait the mouse and therefore draw it in?

- Do you want to detour the mouse from entering in the first place?

- If the mouse is already in the house, is there a particular objection to its presence?

- Could it stay if it were clean?

- Could it stay if it didn't nibble at wires and food?

- If it were housebroken, would it be allowed some space under the floor boards?

Not to mention, the very phrase "build a better mousetrap" has a fair amount of programming, guidance, and limitations built into the very statement itself:

build - verb
  \ 'bild \
  built\ 'bilt \; building
  transitive verb
  1: to form by ordering and uniting materials by gradual means into a composite whole : CONSTRUCT

better - adjective
  bet·ter | \ 'be-tɘr \
  comparative of GOOD
  1: more advantageous or effective. a better solution

mouse - noun
  \ 'maus \
  plural mice\ 'mīs \
  1: any of numerous small rodents (as of the genus Mus) with pointed snout, rather small ears, elongated body, and slender tail

trap - noun
  \ 'trap \
  1: a device for taking game or other animal especially: one that holds by springing shut suddenly

The very description of the challenge precludes any significant innovation.

In contract speak, to fulfill this statement of work, "build a better mousetrap," you must:

- Construct a product or mechanism of some kind.
- It must compare in function and effectiveness to some previous model, a key performance indicator that is not adequately defined.
- Specified target: a "mouse" definition or specification withheld.
- Specified method: "trap" specification of deliverable withheld.

By this definition of innovation, something doesn't qualify unless it is built, better, for mice, and a trap. But this breakdown can cut off other solutions, maybe even the right solution.

- What if you built a mouse fence?
- What if you used an ultrasonic frequency that only mice could hear and hated?
- What if you could hire a medieval piper of some kind to lure all the mice out of town?
- What if you could make the environment such that a mouse wouldn't prefer it?

Or maybe, just maybe, you could make friends with the mouse.

If you could ask it to call first before coming over, or ask it not to nibble the wires, maybe you can find a diplomatic solution to your mouse problem. If only you could make friends with the mouse.

THIS SCENARIO IS MEANT TO SOUND RIDICULOUS

As did a carriage that didn't need a horse. As did phones that didn't require wires, flying like birds, swimming deep like whales, X-rays and the ability to look inside the human body, SONAR and the ability to see without sight. Newton's quest for the Philosopher's Stone seems to the modern ear as ridiculous as if he was trying to describe our eventual landing on the moon to the people of his own time.

By thinking of the ridiculous, by asking questions of the insane, you open up possibilities that are immediately limited with statements like "build a better mousetrap."

True innovation is to consider that instead of building a better mouse trap, you could make friends with the mouse.

CHAPTER NINE

ISN'T "NEPOTISM" A TYPE OF ICE CREAM?

———

TL;DR—We disregard and misdefine facts constantly. People ignore truth because it came from someone they don't like or is associated with the wrong thing. If we redefine the parameters around a problem, we will often find the solution. We have to be willing to accept alternative viewpoints, perspectives, and even definitions.

YOUR DICTIONARY IS LYING TO YOU

Right now, in your vocabulary, your association, your language you will find a word with a unique perspective to you. Another way to put that is: you will find a word you define "wrong." This phenomenon isn't really anyone's fault; it actually occurs because your dictionary is lying to you.

"Literally" doesn't mean "figuratively," even though some dictionaries would tell you it does. "Decimate" and "annihilate" have distinct historical and etymological differences but are often listed as synonyms. "Irregardless" is a word, with a distinct usage and definition independent of "regardless," and "innovation" and "invention" are actually different even though nearly every dictionary uses them to define each other.

Regional differences, common turns of phrase, background, age, and a myriad of other factors unique to specifically you or your family produce associations to words you aren't always aware of.

Even when we share a common language, a differentiation in perspective separates communication. Rhetorical styles infiltrate and affect our understanding. Sometimes enough that we know our definition is "wrong," but more often two people are using the same word or instruction, without a shared definition or intent … and have no idea.

Shortcuts in our own language divide our understanding. Perspectives in our own background create different realities … and then, unaware of that fact, we try to communicate.

When we don't know it's happening, it creates rifts, anger, and sometimes even contempt. The greatest opportunities occur, however, when we see it. When we recognize a difference in definition, when we can change the parameters, alter the perspective or constraints, we can beat the unbeatable problem.

But, typically, we surf the wave of common/uncommon expectations. Matters that are rarely expressly stated, just assumed.

"Take the trash out" in many (not all) circumstances actually includes a list of subsequent implied tasks:

Take out the trash:

- Remove full bag of trash.
- Replace with empty bag
- Take full bag of trash to [designated location]
AND SOMETIMES—
- Repeat all steps above for the recycling [different dumpster]

Even though taking the bag out of the can and leaving it on the kitchen floor is technically fulfilling the request. (This tactic doesn't work for my children; it won't work for you either.) Whereas some concepts like "trash removal" really are somewhat understood (I have tried and failed to "take out the trash" in several other countries… not universal), some aspects of your home, office, region, industry, and lifestyle are as "common sense" to you as "take out the trash." Except they aren't actually as standard.

Common sense isn't common. Not because people are stupid … but because the world is not nearly as small and homogenous as we seem to believe.

Words are misdefined, common phrases assumed, parameters of assignments just expected, and then the craziness ensues.

WORDS ARE PROGRAMMING

This idea is very nearly not a metaphor. Words are quite literally (NOT figuratively) a major method by which our brain processes data. Words are the associative anchor tied to a visual, emotional, or otherwise construct.

Much like a computer running code, at our base state, we accept the data that we hear and run it. We incorporate our individual association to tropes we understand and experiences we've had, most often in the order in which we heard it.

FUN FACT: Our brains can often "eliminate" parts of the "incoming code" (words or images) that it didn't understand or that seemed to contradict—many times BEFORE we are aware of it.

Meaning: We functionally ignore information that interrupts our understanding.

Simple understanding of this concept and a little self-training can help overcome this particular habit. However, most often it is the natural tendency.

CLICHED CONDITIONING

"Build a better mousetrap" is a watered-down cliché that should not be taken literally. Yet I go pretty far down the rabbit hole with it. Why?

Because "take out the trash" means a lot more than "take out the trash." Phrases contain sub-programming that is "assumed," but isn't universal. The same problem we find with the words and programming of that phrase are actually firmly rooted in our culture and social programming.

We react to "programming" in words, emotions, delivery, and our physical surroundings a lot more subconsciously than we are taught or realize.

I know many entrepreneurs and "innovators" who cling firmly to "inventions" being the cornerstone of "innovation." They must "BUILD" something. They ignore new processes, new methods, new designs ... innovation to them is "NEW STUFF."

We build parameters in our head for what something should be, could be, or is, and we defend or defy anything that falls outside of it. We use entirely irrelevant factors to confirm, refute, or even invalidate claims. We take incomplete instructions and cling to the fragments of guidance given, often completely blind to the voids, and respond only to the insufficient pieces available.

Whether we choose to trust someone because of some subconscious association, or perhaps we choose to disregard their opinion because of how they voted in the last election. Maybe we have to do exactly what our teacher wrote on the chalkboard or we won't get extra recess for "following instructions."

Whether or not we want to believe it, we all respond to verbal and societal programming—in the same way that "build a better mousetrap" is a terrible, nondescriptive phrase that we cling to.

DON'T DO THAT.

We live in a world that is increasingly demanding "credible sources." That request sounds awesome and valid, except it then cherry-picks its own limiting versions of "credible." My experience has taught me that if people can disregard your counterpoint, no matter how valid, for nearly any reason, they will.

To combat this phenomenon, Cambridge suppressed the alchemy works of Sir Isaac Newton, not wanting the great mind to be disregarded as the fantastic whackadoo he sort of was.

Most kids, at some point, start ignoring their parents, because "parents are old and out of touch." Their opinions mean less, because they are parents.

Imagine being Jacob Dylan, lead singer of The Wallflowers, rocking out in your garage with your friends. Your father comes in and says:

"SON! Turn this DOWN!!! Good music doesn't have to be LOUD!!!"

And you retort!

"C'mon, Dad! What would you know about good music?!?!"

For those unfamiliar, Jacob Dylan's father is Bob Dylan—perhaps one of the most iconic folk-rock singer-songwriters in history.[80]

---

80 This scenario is a COMPLETE dramatization, and I have absolutely no
    basis nor reason to believe it is true. I just think the visual is humorous
    and emphasizes my point.

We disregard people for the weirdest reasons. A person's political affiliation, recreational activities, or given lifestyle can massively affect their perceived credibility. The parent/family member example gets even worse if you use it externally.

Again, Jacob Dylan is testing a song with some friends. The friends are hugely critical:

"Jacob, you've missed the mark HARD, this time."

Jacob Dylan says, "Yeah? Well, my dad likes it!" and receives an eye roll from his friends.[81]

But the fact that it's his father for some reason removes the credibility.

People get almost excited to disregard someone's opinion or statement.

I'm pretty sure certain individuals could get up and read the encyclopedia, or direct data from a scientific study, and people would still call them a liar due to some perceived disqualification.

To that end, I was warned against citing or referencing certain people I feature in this book for myriad association reasons: Edison was a jerk and thief, Ford was an anti-Semitist, the Founding Fathers were slave-owners. I was cautioned, repeatedly, against quoting or citing immediate family members, or people with whom I shared a last name.

---

81   Again, no proof this EVER happened.

"Doesn't matter who they are, if it's your family it will undercut the authority and veracity."

—"HELPFUL" ADVICE

But if Isaac Newton can spend a majority of his life chasing after the Philosopher's Stone and still have his lucid moments of brilliance recognized, I'm going to take a shot:

My father spent thirty-three years in the Army. He led soldiers, was a diplomat in the Saudi Ministry of Defense, was lent to several "three-letter-agencies" to conduct sensitive assignments, worked closely with the cabinet of the Queen of England and the presidents of many nations, has personally spoken with the Dalai Lama on multiple occasions, was awarded one of George H.W. Bush's "Thousand Points of Light," and received a fellowship in leadership and group dynamics from Harvard University.

My father is a real American badass. I regret the fruit fell so far from the tree.

MISDEFINE WORDS, REDEFINE ASSIGNMENTS

John Westwood grew up in one of those "Big Cities" in middle America that is only classified as a big city by people who have never been to one. He grew up across the street from a large public cemetery, and to paraphrase his words, every game of tag, baseball, cowboys, cops and robbers, and even the best sledding hill were in that cemetery.

He made friends with the groundskeeper, helped dig graves from time to time, camped (yes, really), and more or less spent the entirety of his youth on the grounds. Camping, sledding, playing, you get the point. Now, if the reading audience is anything like the near dozens of people that I've told this story to over the last decade, your eyes are either quizzically quirked, or your mouth is agape with near horror.

He doesn't see cemeteries the way the rest of us do. His reaction isn't "normal."

When John hears "cemetery," he thinks warm summer nights, baseball, hide-n-seek, Sandlot-esque Americana of mid-century America. For John, a cemetery with green grass and rolling hills evokes the same feeling that Norman Rockwell paintings do for the "normal folk." He has told me that he has to actively remind himself to see it any other way.

We don't share that verbal programming.

Actually, despite John being my father, a person who bequeathed to me a significant number of traits, and a considerable portion of my worldview and upbringing, we don't share perspective on much. I don't just mean the standard "we disagree politically" or other opinion differences. I mean my father has a remarkably unique view on the world and perspective on situations that is, like his view on cemeteries, unique to him.

I have spent much of my life trying to see things the way he does … but can't.

I just know his perspective "works."

Regardless, I disregard my nepotistic warnings for a few reasons.

- First, it is silly advice.
- Recognition earned shouldn't be disregarded due to irrelevant association. That's ridiculous.
- Second, and more importantly:
- His life and unique (some might say "incorrect") perspective proves a point I haven't been able to as concretely frame without including it.

REAL LIFE KOBAYASHI MARU

For those who are not Star Trek-inclined, the Kobayashi Maru was the final exam of Starfleet Academy, a simulation with no "correct" answer. No matter what the person taking the test did, they would "fail."[82]

The idea was that the test let the Academy see how you handled an unwinnable situation. It gauged your actions, your priorities, and your temperament. It is programmed to be

---

82 Nicholas Meyer, William Shatner, Leonard Nimoy, Kirstie Alley (1982). Star Trek II: The Wrath of Khan (DVD). Paramount.

impossible. Defeat is part of the central programming of the simulation. As such, everyone "fails." Except for my namesake, one Captain James T. Kirk.

Before this becomes a novelized, fan fiction or retelling of a story you know better than me, Captain Kirk beat the test. He was able to successfully complete all stated objectives.

He cheated.

Knowing that the simulation was unwinnable, he hacked into the mainframe and changed the parameters of the simulation. Therefore, he did what couldn't be done. He was successful.

His reasoning was that he didn't believe in a "no-win scenario," and when faced with one, he changed what needed to be changed to find success.

To avoid what is certainly a topic for an undergrad ethics class, evaluating what he did as right or wrong isn't the point.

The point is: Every student in Starfleet history saw the simulation within a set of parameters. Often, they went in knowing the situation was "unwinnable" and proceeded anyway. They were tasked to solve a problem presented by someone else, use only the tools they were given, operate only within the scenario as presented, and they failed the task as expected.

Captain Kirk did as he was instructed.

He approached the problem as presented.

He met the objectives as they were expressed.

BUT he did so by approaching the problem from outside the expected and accepted parameters.

He cheated. Others saw the situation within the simulation as the problem and went forward to their inevitable defeat.

Captain Kirk saw the simulation as the problem.

This approach has a drastically different set of parameters and objectives. Those he was able to influence. He started where everyone else did. But he looked at the problem a bit differently.

THE COLD WAR IN ALL ITS AMBIGUITY

For nearly fifty years, the United States was posturing for the clear incoming conflict with the USSR. Our military swelled in size, our defensive and offensive posture circumnavigated the globe, and combatant troops stood, just waiting for the word "go."

One such soldier was a young Air Defense artillery commander, Captain John S. Westwood.

Due to the reality of the threat, units were stationed all across Europe. They trained relentlessly, keeping up their guard to what was perceived to be a very real inevitability.

Annually, each unit was inspected against a remarkably thorough and detailed list of requirements. Each section was inventoried, each commander graded. This situation wasn't just "war games"; it was very much the real thing:

Are you and your men ready to fight?

To "fail" one of these examinations was not a small problem. In fact, it most likely signaled the end or significant derailment of your career. To pass was difficult but expected, and to receive "exemplary" marks wasn't expected, as it was set to be near impossible.

Across the fifteen graded sections, most commanders hoped to get one or two "exemplary" remarks. Captain Westwood got twelve, three years in a row, and received scores that gave his unit honors placing them as the best in Europe, twice.

He not just passed the test, but as a man who was barely thirty, he dominated. He did what had never been done before; he cleaned house on a test with expectations so high, barely passing was intended to be difficult.

He "cheated."

I'll explain.

In the military, there are set sections, then within those sections set jobs, and when you join the military you are given a Military Occupational Specialty (MOS), which designates you the owner of a set category or line of responsibilities.

Every unit is built on paper with a set number of sections, a set number of positions in each section, and the MOS required for that position. Like a table of contents for every unit, when a problem happens, finding whose responsibility it was is actually quite easy. From unit to unit, a set standard exists. These sections have these people, with these MOS's, and they operate in this way. Done.

In many ways, this phenomenon was the paradigm that the annual inspection was testing. Or, more accurately, this was the framework and these the assumptions that the evaluators were operating under.

To fix problems within this framework, you go to a section, identify the squeaky wheel or inefficiency and you fix it. You operate from section to section. You provide guidance and feedback to section by section. This process is how you cleaned house.

But an inherent problem arises with this approach. Much like the Kobayashi Maru, it doles out a problem, a solution, and a system and sequence, and it offered judgment based on a standardized expectation that may not fit based on numerous conditions.

The first of which was, as the Army shuffles constantly, teams are trained somewhat asymmetrically. Despite best efforts to the contrary, you could end up with a very lopsided set of soldiers as far as skills and abilities go. Like having two less experienced soldiers in a section with no one to guide them, and another section with nothing but rock stars, then being told to operate within that standard with your metaphorical hands tied behind your back.

Making chicken salad out of chicken sh!t

With all the other accolades and accomplishments of Col. Westwood (RET), more than any of the things that could be and were said and sung of his accomplishments, none were to be overshadowed by the phrase I saw engraved or inscribed on every gift, plaque, or award he was ever given. "You Can't Make a Chicken Salad out of Chicken Shit."

I can't tell you where it started, but I can tell you it was because of stories like this one. Being asked to produce a product with no resources, inadequate support, and regulations preventing anything resembling a solution wasn't something John Westwood would accept:

Captain Westwood didn't like this "no-win" condition. From his perspective, he obviously had soldiers of vastly asymmetrical skill sets, often misaligned with the most difficult tasks. He had an abundance of qualified individuals, but they were not always the "right kind" of soldiers. He also, like every organization, had soldiers who were far less capable and skilled. As luck would have it, they were the soldiers who were often the official key holder over some of the most heavily weighted sections of the annual evaluation.

For example, a mechanic from the motor pool with a near neurological attention to detail being one of several amazing mechanics, but "supply" has only two soldiers in charge of inventory and order of the quartermaster's storage and neither is very strong at paperwork or organization.

So, he fixed it.

He found ways within the system and recognized organization to move skilled soldiers out of their designated section and job distinction, into areas where they were on paper "unqualified." He assigned "assistants" to some of the soldiers who were struggling. They didn't need to feel removed from their own bailiwick nor given a babysitter. But who wouldn't like some help?

While the nature of the evaluation on paper was to grade the quality of your designated sections and staff and the manner in which they functioned, it held his resources where they weren't needed, and left other areas in definitive need for help. He changed the parameters of the assignment, at least as far as traditionally held.

A review with fifteen sections, "satisfactory" being a difficult standard and "exemplary" designed to be near mythological, the Kobayashi Maru, the unwinnable situation. But if you change the parameters of the test, anything is possible.

2003—THE INVASION OF IRAQ—THE WORLD AT WAR

In researching the military and their approach to innovation, I came across another rock star and story, with a similar situation. We'll see him a few times in the chapters to follow, but here is the first.

Major General James "Boe" Young was commissioned in 1983 as an intelligence officer out of Davidson College. Much can be said about his career, and much has been. As with anyone who ascends to the rank of major general (two stars), his career was filled with distinction and merit.

In 2003, he was a lieutenant colonel tasked with leading a group of soldiers. This duty is well within a military officer's job description, but three things stood out as different with this particular tasking.

- a. This group was "Joint Service," which is to say that some members of the team weren't in the Army, but rather the Air Force or one of the other sister services.
- b. This group was multinational, meaning it had ranking officers not just from the US Army, but Australia and England as well.
- c. The requirements of their mission were not supported by the experience and capabilities of the members of the team.
- d. It's nice to hear that even twenty years after Cpt. Westwood was having this struggle, it remained unfixed by the military.

THEIR ASSIGNMENT:

Target and identify weapons of mass destruction, equipment brought into the country in violation of UN sanctions, or equipment modified to do something different than it was designed to …

This group of largely intelligence officers was brilliant by any academic standard. Ltc. Young was the commander, his superior being an Australian Brigadier general equivalent (one star). Members of the task force held advanced degrees in diverse fields, their military and civilian experience having distinguished them as leading experts in various technologies, armaments, capabilities, etc.

Their mission required significant "field trips" into what was considered the active war zone. MG Young recalls the access and mobility of Iraq was less permissive than they had assumed. They were all trained soldiers, but none of their core competency was direct engagement warfighting. They were not tactical officers.

This reality created a paradox in the mission: the design of the unit wasn't right for the mission of the unit. The group had one set of competencies to complete the functional half of the mission, but not the resources or support to complete the logistical part.

This unit design would have been appropriate in a different context, but was not the correct makeup for the task at hand. Now it was up to the commander to handle it.

MG YOUNG RECOUNTED THE SITUATION

"[We had] a lot of people that had never gone out on a combat mission before, I mean, literally … [we had a] PhD, that was the smartest guy in the world in terms of communications gear [or] missile technology, but you weren't sure he knew the right end of the rifle. Likewise, you had senior officers from other services who were used to being in charge."

The structures and traditions of the military are the oldest standing archetypes in US history. Military ranks, the status they evoke, and the hard-earned insignia they display are often near sacrosanct to people who have them. But just as Cpt. Westwood had found in Cold War-era Germany, it takes misaligning some resources to make it work.

"I convinced the brigade commander to give me long range surveillance company out of the National Guard, infantry men supposed to be doing long range surveillance, but there was really no mission for that, at this point."

"They came to me as my force protection muscle, they were infantry, with gun jeeps, and MK-18s" (better rifles than M16s).

Then we had the problem of the military paradox: certain individuals with the rank to lead, but not the experience— OR—the soldiers with the experience and qualifications, but not the position, seniority, or rank. All nested within an organization with heavy traditions, and written regulations dictating how to operate, that are wholly inadequate to handle the idiosyncrasies of the situation.

"We came up with a different construct that created … two leadership positions for every mission. There was the mission commander, and … the security commander."

"The security commander was always the infantry guy, and the mission commander was not always the senior person. [The mission commander] was the person that did the planning on the mission, the routes, how many people are going to go, which buildings, we're going to look at, what was the equipment we're looking for, etc.

"We created a construct, that allowed us to execute our mission. What would have been more typical would be the senior persons in charge. But in our case that could have meant, an Air Force Colonel [that had] never ridden in a Humvee before… leading a mission into a combat zone…

"But ours could have had an Army Lieutenant and Army Sergeant in charge of a mission. IN CHARGE, like 'sit down and do what you're told, **COLONEL**.'

'We had … colonels who were rifleman, majors who were rifleman, being led by sergeants and lieutenants. It was a different way to approach a problem and turned out to be pretty successful."

"Let me 'splain … No, there is too much. Let me sum up."

—INIGO MONTOYA, THE PRINCESS BRIDE, 1987

Two examples separated by decades within the same organization. Both created success by redefining the paradigm. Changing the expected structure. Operating outside of expected definitions of the construct. In writing and reading both these stories, I'll say that their solutions seem so straightforward they don't strike me as noteworthy.

I'll say that I've found the solution is actually almost always that simple, but hidden behind two things:

Incorrect perceptions of a situation caused by poor communication or alternative understandings of what was meant.

—or—

Navigating the egos and experience of the team members.

Both are actually far more difficult than tackling the complexities of the actual problem.

The words we don't have a common definition for, our tendency to invalidate people for irrelevant reasons, expected structures, and assumed associated tasks: all are standardized things weakened by the standard they are judged by.

Perceptions, experience, and perceived "expertise" are actually what make us brilliant, but they are and can also be the biggest liability to our progress. For example, potentially disregarding a decorated military diplomat because he happens to be my father.

CHAPTER TEN

LATERAL THINKING OF WITHERED TECHNOLOGY

TL;DR—Gunpei Yokoi invented the Game and Watch and Gameboy using outdated tech. This innovation of looking at things differently kept him ahead of the competitors using the newest technology. This concept applied to my company saved us significant ongoing capital and resulted in capabilities not currently available on the market.

TECHNOLOGY SEPARATES US, OR MORE, IT DEFINES US IN WAYS WE DON'T ANTICIPATE

Something that stands as a true differentiator between generations and groups is the technology available to them at key ages.

STORY TIME

I was born in 1982. Growing up, cell phones were something that people knew about but they weren't common. In high school, my parents bought a car that had a built-in car phone and we all thought it was awesome. At eighteen, just out of high school, my job required me to go get a real-life cell phone. It was the year 2000: I bought an AT&T Nokia flip phone on which I would play Brick and Snake until my hand cramped up.

As a point of comparison, my oldest daughter, who was born in 2007, is now in middle school and has an iPhone.

A moment of parental defensiveness: I did NOT buy her an iPhone. It was an old one we had in the house. I didn't think she really needed a phone, being twelve, but the number of times I showed up to pick her up from dance to find out they'd moved it, or were going to be going long, or something, and had to be informed by another parent who had received the text from their ten-year-old an hour ago ... I caved ... but this all goes to my point. Technology separates us ... or, again, more accurately, defines us.

Was your signal for when to be home the streetlights going on? Mine was.

Have you or anyone you loved repeatedly died of dysentery? I have.

Have you ever filled up your car and gotten change back from your $10? Those were the days.

We tend to use the capabilities of an era to define it.

We tend to use our association with technology to help place a timeline.

A fictional conversation you have had or heard:

Person 1: *"It would have had to be in the mid-'90s; I remember because we were using dial-up."*

Person 2: *"No, that can't be right, because I had a cell phone, and we had DSL by the time I had a cell phone."*

Or maybe it was the 8-Track/Cassette/CD/MP3/Bluetooth phone that was playing the music in the car.

We tend to divide up our lives by technology, which is yet another reason that, when thinking of innovation, people tend to immediately think, what new thing can I invent? That's how we benchmark our timeline, and therefore the "only" way you could change the world.

EXCEPT ...

We can see a few problems with this thinking. First and foremost, it places us solidly in the consumer mind frame. It allows us to define our era based on the capabilities of things that were available for us to purchase and utilize within our sphere of influence. It makes "innovation" synonymous with "Can I buy it at Best Buy?" or probably "Amazon"—or worse, "as seen on TV."

Innovations and inventions are separate and distinct. Where the matter gets more confusing is that invention sometimes requires innovation, which of course further conflates the non-synonyms. However, innovation isn't "What new thing can I build?" Innovation should be far more simply defined as: "How can I use what I already have to do this better?"

Chandler: Why do we use the little twinkle lights? I remember we used to use the great BIG ones!
Rachel: That's a great story, Grandpa.

—FRIENDS SEASON 6

THE HERO YOU'VE (PROBABLY) NEVER HEARD OF

If you are a hardcore gamer (which I am NOT), you may have heard the name. If you aren't, possibly not, but either way, Gunpei Yokoi[83] seems to cover the whole of modern game design. Details about the life of this Nintendo designer outside of his accomplishments are sparse, and even many dedicated gamers fail to grasp the sheer innovation and genius of this man, who is responsible for not just technological innovation, but seeding pieces of ongoing modern culture.

Gunpei was born in Kyoto, Japan, in September of 1941, shortly before the country entered World War II. He was the son of a successful director of a pharmaceutical company, and although little is known about Gunpei's childhood, we do know in 1965 he graduated Doshisha University in Kyoto with a degree in electronics. Heading out into postgraduate world,

---

83 "Gunpei Yokoi." 2020. Nintendo.

he found work as a technician, maintaining assembly-line and production equipment, at the small, family-owned, playing card company Nintendo.[84]

A hobbyist and creator in his spare time, Yokoi was known to take spare parts and craft gadgets and toys, if for no other reason than his own amusement.

Due to a sharp downturn in the playing card industry, Nintendo was struggling financially and needed something to change, if the family-owned company was to stay afloat. President Hiroshi Yamauchi came to Yokoi in 1970 and charged him with making something, ANYTHING, for Christmas.

Without additional funding of note, nor a team of dedicated engineers, Yokoi developed a simple machine made of wooden lattice and hinge pins, which would allow for simple games of picking things up, called: the Ultra Hand.

Some spare parts and some spare time resulted in a Christmas sensation, with 1.2 million units sold!

Yokoi was immediately moved from his job maintaining production equipment to research and development of the new department simply named Toys. While there, Yokoi was responsible for a long list of inventions and breakaway products. Each, much like the Ultra Hand, were made on principles of simplicity, efficiency, and at the end of the day, fun.

---

84 "As Game Boy Turns 30, It's Time to Recognize Its Inventor, Nintendo's Maintenance Man." 2020. Fortune.

Despite the success of his many inventions, by 1980 the toy market had a looming cloud overhead, with the raging storm of video games on the horizon. Children's toys had lost their footing to the rise in arcades and the home game console.

Sitting on a train heading home one night, after a long day's work, Gunpei noticed a fellow passenger passing the time by punching keys on an LCD calculator. We don't have an account of what exactly the man was doing, but I like to imagine him attempting to spell out words, using combinations of digits in various orientations, despite the fact that the language/alphabet barrier makes this possibility extremely unlikely.

Gunpei reportedly mused, If this man can keep himself entertained with a calculator, what if I could develop an actual game using similarly common, simple, and inexpensive tech?

At this moment Yokoi devised the idea for the Game and Watch, and ultimately the Game Boy was born.

Using nothing but the guts and an LCD display of a calculator, Gunpei developed a device that housed a single game, set against an invariable printed backdrop, which allowed for simple programming to develop a rich host of games including: Ball, Popeye, Mickey Mouse, Snoopy Tennis, Donkey Kong, Mickey & Donald, Black Jack, Zelda, Mario Bros, Super Mario Bros, and many others.

With this new gaming system, came the first "D-Pad"—a cross-shaped arrangement of pressure switches (calculator keys)—as Yokoi knew that a joystick would make the device too big and bulky to be adequately portable. The D-pad alone would be in some way copied or emulated in nearly every game controller to present.

Much like with his previous inventions, he used what amounted to spare parts, easily understood and accessible technology, and programming well within the standards and expectations of the time, to develop something new, something entirely different. His creation was an "invention." But he innovated using old, antiquated tech to make it.

The Game and Watch was new, different, somewhat revolutionary, and involved absolutely no breakthrough technology. It was in production for eleven years, with ten different release series, over twenty original games, and touted over forty-three million units sold. The madness was clearly a success, but the method wasn't fully codified until the Game Boy a few years later.

Much like the Game and Watch, it used a simple display, a D-Pad, and two gameplay buttons with two system buttons. It touted a cartridge-based gaming system that allowed for a multitude of games on a single device, unlike the single game "Game and Watch."

The tech world was all abuzz with the new-fangled "microchip" technology taking off across all sectors, and portable gaming was hardly limited to Nintendo. New processors, new graphics engines, and better technical specs across almost all parts of the platform were available, and many competitors were anxiously and actively developing tech with them.

The competition was tight, the dash to the finish clear, and to most tech developers this rivalry could have been perceived as a cutthroat arms race. The executives at Nintendo were no exception to that emotional response. But Yokoi was confident in one thing: this competition wasn't going to be about the cutting-edge tech. This race was for the future of gaming.

While everyone else was pouring money into the most sophisticated technological gaming system of tomorrow, Gunpei Yokoi wanted to make a better way to play a game. The GAME came first. Everything was there to serve the GAME. If the game was good, you didn't need the distraction of the bells and whistles of technology that didn't yet have the infrastructure or historical experience to support it.

In a 1997 interview looking back at this time of development, Yokoi recalled:

"The technology was there to do color. But I wanted us to do black and white anyway. If you draw two circles on a blackboard, and say "that's a snowman," everyone who sees it will sense the white color of the snow, and everyone will intuitively recognize it's a snowman. That's because we live in a world of information, and when you see that drawing of the snowman, the mind knows this color has to be white.

"I became confident of this after I tried playing some Famicom games on a black and white TV. Once you start playing the game, the colors aren't important. You get drawn, mentally, into the world of the game.

"Actually, it was difficult to get Nintendo to understand [this]. Partly, I used my status in the company to push them into it (he laughs). After we released the Game Boy, one of my staff came to me with a grim expression on his face: 'there's a new handheld on the market similar to ours...' The first thing I asked was: '"is it a color screen, or monochrome?' He told me it was color, and I reassured him, 'Then we're fine.'"[85]

Gunpei Yokoi didn't look at problems the same as others. As such, he didn't see solutions in the same light either. He coined this methodology "lateral thinking of withered technology." Instead of racing for traditional "innovation" and to be the team to invent the newest, biggest, brightest toy, Yokoi wanted to utilize tech that was stable, understood, low-cost, and easily accessed.

By using "withered technology," not only did he keep his costs at a fraction of his competition's, but through "lateral thinking" he was innovating with tech for uses outside its original purpose. This approach provided stable, predictable, low-cost "inventions" powered by fundamental innovation.

---

85   "Console Gaming Then and Now: A Fascinating 1997 Interview With Nintendo's Legendary Gunpei Yokoi." 2015. TechSpot.

The first question that springs to the mind of any enterprising entrepreneur: "Why would it be a good thing that the competitor's product was objectively 'better'?"

To which Yokoi responded:

"When we were designing the Game Boy hardware, we took into consideration what kind of software was going to be made for it, and I think that approach resulted in a very efficient product. Hardware design isn't about making the most powerful thing you can."

Yokoi knew that the color processor, while beautiful, next-generation tech with a "superior processor," also drew significantly more power. It required a number of expensive, nonrechargeable batteries, for a relatively insignificant amount of time (at the time of release, the Atari Lynx required six AA batteries to run for approximately four hours of gameplay). This gimmick of a futuristic feature was a distraction from the quality of the game and literally drained the life from the user experience.

"Today most hardware design is left to other companies., Yokoi *said in his 1997 interview, "but when you make hardware without taking into account the needs of the eventual software developers, you end up with bloated hardware full of pointless excess. From the outset, one must consider design from both a hardware and software perspective."*

"Lateral thinking of withered technology" remains at the forefront of Nintendo design methodology to this day, yet Gunepi Yokoi left Nintendo in 1996. While Xbox and PlayStation duke it out at who can be the best multifaceted super-liquid-cooled, overpowered engine of recreation, Nintendo uses lower-cost processors, nonrealistic graphics, and controllers powered by simple accelerometers, to position itself again as a different experience, unconcerned with its competition.

This concept empowers innovation with what is available. It begs you not to reinvent the wheel, but to find something else the wheel can be used for. Yokoi invites you to question the use of everything—be it lattice strips and hinge pins or calculator screens and simple pressure switches.

LATERAL THINKING BUILDS A STUDIO

Everyone has the basic tools they need to do their job … and every job is different. You know what those things are. You know what those drawbacks are:

An Uber driver needs a car,

An IT professional needs a computer,

A carpenter needs a hammer,

The list goes on …

I work in media production, and with the rise of podcasts and video streaming, I wanted the ability to run a three-camera news/talk show from my facility, so I needed a full studio in my office.

I built one. It is equipped with all the toys, tools, and tricks you'd find at a broadcast news station.

When I initially told the engineers what I needed, they came back with a price breakdown. My options started at a basic $50k and went to near infinite.

They also told me the studio would require a bare minimum of five designated staff/talent to run it to full capacity, and three people to run it at all. My response was "That's not going to work; we need it to cost less."

These engineers were no joke—they had unbelievable and almost unmatched experience, and they tried very hard to remain unpatronizing as they explained to me the costs of the equipment I was asking for, the requirements of running them proficiently, and the drawbacks and pitfalls of "skimping" where it mattered in building a studio.

"Boy, do I hear you," I replied, "but we need it to cost less."

Thus began the multi-month "spirited conversation" (read: argument) in "the way studios work."

A MIXTURE OF MONTHS OF CONVERSATIONS PARAPHRASED FOR EMPHASIS (AND HUMOR)

Them: Kirk, seriously, that's just what these things take. It requires a significant investment to do this well.

Me: I understand that, but what are "these things"? To my knowledge, a full studio dedicated to streaming doesn't exist, so what are you using for a baseline?

Them: A studio is a studio; if you want this to look and feel like a real talk show, we have to model it after the way that it's done.

Me: Perfectly logical. Except it would imply there is only ONE way to get "this done," and that is a premise I'm not sure I can get behind.

Them: What do you want us to cut?

Me: The cost.

Them: Then we'll have to lose some capability!

Me: Nope! Cut something else.

Them: There is nothing else to cut. What you want done is very simple; it just requires very specific people and equipment to get it done.

Me: No ... it takes specific people and equipment to get it done the way you know how to do it. Find a different way.

Them: ... ... (This is usually where my incredulousness and their frustration would end the conversation).

Let me cut to the end: my studio has 99 percent of the capabilities of any television studio in the world and 150 percent of some. It requires two people to run it at full capacity, and those people CAN be the talent on screen. It requires only ONE person to run it if that person isn't on camera.

Let's do the breakdown!

THE LIGHTING GRID:
In truth, you can find a lot of ways to suspend lights from the ceiling. They all require some fairly legitimate infrastructure, rigging, and/or equipment. To build a "real" studio grid the size we wanted, we were quoted $8k, $11k, and $15k.

Lucky for me, I've been working in event and show production as a hobby/side hustle since I was thirteen. "Schedule 40" pipe is a very common tool used for making "lighting trees" or "goal posts," which are just fancy ways of saying stable, yet modular, lighting elements for rooms otherwise ill-equipped.

Schedule 40 pipe isn't used in television studios; its primary use is in construction, and it can be picked up at any hardware store. It is a legitimate, safe, and legal way to hang thousands of pounds of equipment. It just isn't a tool often used by studio engineers, or those who fabricate lighting grids.

The "real" way of doing studio lighting involved modifications to our building, infrastructural changes, electricians, carpenters, and thousands of dollars of specialty equipment to handle and power the lights.

We built ours from Home Depot for $490.

THE CAMERAS:

The original quote provided included new cameras to tackle lots of problems and "future-proof" the studio. But Gunpei covered this matter: hardware without the considerations of software creates bloat. We didn't know everything we would ever do with the studio, but we knew what we'd do most. It didn't need "future proofing"; it needed HD cameras with either an HDMI or SDI connection (if you aren't a nerd, don't worry about that part).

We work in media production. We had several cameras that for various reasons were no longer suitable for our standard engagement that would work fine for this project. We had two FS100u cameras that matched, but we knew we wanted three. The Fs100 is an "old" camera (circa 2011), so we were able to get one off eBay for $450 (we paid $3k each in 2011).

THE SWITCHER:

Exact same as the cameras. We had an old one that was largely out of service.

THE AUDIO:

This is one of the very few items we purchased when we didn't "have to." Much like the cameras and switcher, we had old audio boards that would work just fine, which we used while prototyping. But due to a range of factors, the board had to "live" over with the switcher/cameras/tech. But I wanted the person on camera to have control. Luckily, digital boards with Bluetooth/Wi-Fi controls are readily available, and for around $600 we were able to get an audio board with an iPad interface. Now, the person sitting at the table, if need be, could adjust audio manually, or through an array of presets.

KIBBLES AND BITS:

Without droning on and boring the non-nerds, a lot of random doodads are required to make this stuff work. Some are really cheap at $4. Some aren't, at $300 to $400. Some can be ordered from a store; some require a soldering iron and a basic knowledge in "how this stuff works."

But at the end of the day, we have a functioning studio, which meets and exceeds all our original requirements. It was made of discarded "irrelevant" pieces, garbage, "the wrong materials," and the as of yet to be truly explained "misaligned memories" of tools used in irrelevant industries to build.

We finished this project for 10 percent of the stated cost.

The other way to say that is we cut 90 percent of the estimate.

We used an understanding of what we needed versus what our contractors understood.

We used a lateral thinking of withered technology.

AN EARLY CONCLUSION: TAKEN TOO SOON:

A year after leaving Nintendo, Gunpei and his driver were in a small fender bender on a road in Japan. When Gunpei got out to assess the damage, a passing car struck him, and he died from his injuries a few hours later, at only fifty-six years old.[86]

The enigmatic legacy of Gunpei Yokoi surrounds and encapsulates nearly the entirety of the gaming industry. His contribution to both technology and culture through his innovation and game titles, even when they're not actively talked about, remain a part of daily life for millions of people around the world.

Gunpei Yokoi used creative problem-solving and innovation to fuel the invention that changed the world, not by building a better mousetrap, but by considering an alternative use for the mouse.

Lateral thinking of withered technology.

Gunpei, wherever you are, you are my hero.

---

86 "Gunpei Yokoi, Chief Designer of Game Boy, Is Dead at 56."
    2020. Nytimes.Com.

CHAPTER ELEVEN

DON'T REINVENT THE WHEEL

———

TL;DR—We need to reinvent the wheel; it has been reinvented thousands of times, and we don't want to be the person not trying. Alec Issigonis designed The Mini to almost impossible specifications. Frank Stephenson brought it the future by using the past.

On the list of statements I love to hate, "Don't reinvent the wheel" has to be one of my absolute favorites. I know I've breezed past this point a few times, and I don't want to bore you, but this statement, for all its axiomatic applications, needs to stop.

We should always be looking for new efficiencies.

However, much like the subtle programming of "build a better mousetrap," "don't reinvent the wheel" sets an expectation and precedent that we shouldn't actually want. If the person saying it DOES in fact want those sentiments and precedents, that's when things get murky.

But first, let's start with a deeply flawed and incomplete history from a non-historian: me.

THE WHEEL

An imperfect and incomplete history of man's most vital invention:

The wheel is old. REALLY old. Which is to say our first recordings of its existence begin around 3500 BCE, approximately the same time as our first introductions to recorded history. But the wheel is often thought of, or at least discussed as if it was, near the top of the to-do list of early mankind:

8 a.m.—Learn to walk without using hands.

9:30 a.m.—Figure out some way to heat cave, cook food, and provide light.

10:15 a.m.—Develop some sweet rims for my push wagon to make it more dope.

Not that I really need to point this out, but the wheel's invention didn't really go down like that.

In fact, due to discrepancies in dating technology, methods of recording history, and the vast array of civilizations and use of wheels, the story gets pretty murky as to who invented what and when. But 3500 BCE seems to be the most prevailing number.

You should actually know four really interesting things about the wheel:

1. IT IS THE FIRST, AND VERY MUCH ONE OF THE ONLY, FUNDAMENTAL INVENTIONS NOT DERIVED FROM NATURE.

Boats are an invention to mimic a variety of animals that float, skim, or travel over/in water. Birds inspired the plane. Forks and pitchforks were derived from using naturally forked sticks. Ropes were just ways of replicating vines. Even fabrics and cloth, which could be a derivative of wearing leather skins as clothing, are somewhat naturally occurring, as matted hair of animals producing early felt.

But the wheel? Nope. Doesn't exist in nature. Outside of a rock rolling down a hill, we can't see any natural occurrences of the wheel.

2. IN THE INVENTIONS OF MAN, THE WHEEL COMES A LOT LATER THAN PEOPLE REALIZE.

Many unique Homo sapiens and advanced tools were developed before the wheel. Weaving reeds and sticks to make baskets, rope, woven cloth, needles, fishhooks—they all came before the wheel.

It was the Bronze Age. They had canals, cultivated crops, domesticated animals, sailboats, harps and flutes, even the forging of metal tools using alloys. Not to be oversimplifying nor over-congratulatory, but this fact would imply that humans understood irrigation, animal husbandry, basic meteorology, music theory, and chemistry BEFORE the wheel.

3. THE FIRST RECORDED EVIDENCE OF A WHEEL WASN'T FOR TRANSPORTATION; IT WAS FOR POTTERY.

To reemphasize my point, the collecting of clay, shaping of it, correct firing of it, and use of it for containers, a relatively complicated process, all happened before the wheel.[87]

4. THE WHEEL IS NOT THE INVENTION THAT IS INTERESTING OR ALL THAT IMPORTANT. (SEE CHAPTER: CREDIT MISFILED)

The actual breakthrough that changed the world was the axle.[88] Wheels spinning independently of a fixed rod are what made the potter's wheel, the chariot, and the Maserati possible.

---

87 Megan Gambino 2009. "A Salute to the Wheel." Smithsonian Magazine.

88 Natalie Wolchover, 2012. "Why It Took So Long to Invent the Wheel." Livescience.Com.

PLEASE REINVENT THE WHEEL; EVERYONE ELSE HAS.

The wheel started as a solid disk with a hole in it. Depending on whose history you lean into, spokes would take another 1,000 years: 2200 BCE (ish).

The addition of spokes made the wheel far more stable, able to hold more weight, better balanced, and capable of consistency to the wheels themselves.

- Around 1000 BCE, the marginal improvement of iron rims was added to better hold it all together.
- In the early 1800s, wire spokes were added.
- 1845 saw the first pneumatic rubber wheels by R.W. Thompson.
- In 1885, Dunlop reinvented the pneumatic rubber wheel, using his better rubber process.

—also—

- 1885: Karl Benz developed the first wheel for an automobile.
- In 1910, B.F. Goodrich added carbon to the rubber to increase strength.
- 1927: Steel-welded spoked tires entered the scene.[89,90,91]
- At this point, the history becomes hard to track, because reinventing the wheel became a pretty popular thing to do.

89 Engineering, Interesting, Trevor English, Ariella Brown, Christopher McFadden, and Christopher McFadden. 2017. "The History and Evolution of the Wheel." Interestingengineering.Com.
90 "Invention of the Wheel - Timeline Index." 2020. Timelineindex.Com.
91 "The Wheel Timeline." 2020. Timetoast.

Dozens of tire companies, various galvanization processes, steels, alloys, milled, forged, cast. We could easily dismiss these as not "reinventions" of the wheel, but rather innovations on better ways to make one, or to make wheels more efficient.

And that mind-set very well may be true. But ask yourself this: The last time you were told "don't reinvent the wheel," would the author of the statement have been satisfied if you told them you were simply aiming for innovation on better ways to make one, or make the aforementioned wheel more efficient?

In my experience, no. That phrase is used by people assured of their own superiority to ask you to do things their way, or at least "the way things are supposed to be done."

But "reinventing the wheel" should absolutely be a vital part of our brainstorming process. We don't know where opportunities and inefficiencies lie. The way we figure that out is often by reevaluating our basic assumptions.

THE PAST ESTABLISHED THE PRESENT AND IS THE BEST ROADMAP TO THE FUTURE.

As we discussed in "Chapter 10: Lateral Thinking of Withered Technology," the many systems that failed were those that reached to the cutting-edge, next-generation tech, wanting to break the technological mold! The true successful product was the one that didn't reach to tomorrow's technology, but yesterday's technology.

STORY TIME [92,93,94]

The year was 1957, and the man's name was Alec Issigonis. He was an engineer for the Morris Company, and his employer Sir Leonard Percy Lord, 1st Baron Lambury KBE, issued him a task that would have some fairly significant cultural ramifications.

Gas prices were soaring. World War II wasn't too far in the rearview mirror, and the Suez Crisis wasn't even really "history" yet. The circumstances left a lot of people unsure if owning or maintaining the available cars of the time was worth it, or if they needed to explore other options.

Sir Leonard Lord wanted a solution for the people of Britain. The challenge issued was far from simple: a small, fuel-efficient car that could fit four adults and be affordable for essentially anyone who wanted one. To keep the price point where it needed to be and the fuel economy where it had to be, inventing something new, custom, or fancy was out of the question. Alec Issigonis was going to have to use what he had available to reinvent the automobile.

HE STARTED WITH THE WHEELS

To maximize space inside the car for four adults, the wheel placement would need to be a little unconventional. They were

---

92   Boeriu, Horatiu. 2012. "The History of the MINI Cooper." BMW BLOG

93   "History of MINI – Story, Heritage & Origins – MINI USA." 2020. MINI USA.

94   Trotta, Mark. 2020. "Classic Mini History." Classic-Car-History.Com.

pushed to the far corners of the small frame. Not only did this give the requisite space for passengers, it also afforded amazing stability and wide posture on its small frame.

The next problem was the engine itself. Engines being shaped the way they are, and with no real ability to redesign the combustion engine from scratch, Issigonis had to find a way to fit the engine in the tiny space without removing what would need to be leg room.

Sideways. No reinventions. Nothing earth-shattering, nor inconceivable … just never really done before. He put the engine in sideways. Some logistical reasons favor having the engine situated "the way it is supposed to be," but strictly speaking, no requirement exists. Placing the engine in laterally or, as some would call it, "wrong" maximized the space at the front.

Tiny modifications in "the standard practice," reinventions and re-situations of existing components in functional, but unconventional ways, and restrictive requirements for size, price, and fuel efficiency set the bar fairly high. And when THE MINI hit streets in 1959, nobody knew what to think or do with it.

BUT IT DIDN'T TAKE LONG

Very soon the MINI became a symbol for independence and a free spirit. It transcended class and was equally adopted by the down-and-outs and the distinguished, from the "right-on" rocker to the royal family.

An unquestioning cultural phenomenon, the MINI remained in production without update or significant change for forty years. But laws and production standards were looming, and in the 1990s the word came down from the powers that be: significant changes would be required to keep the MINI in production into the new millennium.

HOW DO WE GET THERE FROM HERE?

By 1994, the ownership of the MINI brand had changed hands and landed with none other than German auto-phenom BMW. The decision lay at their feet:

Did they bow to upcoming legislation and let the MINI fade from the lineup, or did they update and create the twenty-first-century MINI? That was their challenge.

The pressure was on for a variety of reasons. No executive wants to be helming the ship when you run aground a cultural phenomenon of close to a half-century. You can't disregard a flagship vehicle in your lineup, but most of all, you can't be the one in charge of screwing it up.

They decided to move forward, but knew they couldn't make a mistake.

Their design process was going to be a little unconventional; they wanted options, top-quality options—fifteen, to be exact.

Not wanting to make a mistake, they opened up a design competition worldwide. Instead of doing the normal two or three design proposals, they enlisted fifteen designers from all around the world to come at it from different angles.

… and so, with six months to produce a complete redesign of the new MINI, fifteen designers started conceptualizing.

A REMARKABLY LARGE MINI LINEUP

In October 1995, fifteen new MINIs, all the same length car, but with otherwise original designs, were fanned out in front of the executive board of BMW and Rover. They were there to choose the new MINI.

The designers had not been allowed to speak to each other during the six months. They were prohibited from knowing what their colleagues were doing. They arrived that day to the decision makers, and for the first time saw fourteen other would-be MINIs.

Frank Stephenson, the designer of the chosen new MINI, recounted of the day, "I could see in a lot of the design proposals … 95 percent of them, that the designers had gone off on a whim and designed a car that would be called the new MINI." He went on to say the other fourteen cars had little visual or emotional connection to its history. "Nothing that you could say, 'That's the original MINI from '59 designed in a modern way.'"

And nobody approached the project like Frank did.

I'm not a car designer myself, and I can't say I've ever had to tackle a project like redefining a beloved classic for the modern era while balancing nostalgic charm and modern sensibilities. I'm not sure how I would approach such a task. But I'm confident of one thing: Frank's way wouldn't have occurred to me.

The MINI was the MINI for forty years. The shape of the car, the look, and the size were constant—some small trim changes, a few minor variations, but essentially unchanged. This situation is relatively uncommon, especially for that length of time: for a car to remain unmodified.

THE HISTORY IS WHERE FRANK STARTED

For the first month of his process, he did not start designing a modern MINI as his assignment. Instead, he gave the MINI its missing traditional update schedule.

"I had four weeks [for] research. What I did the first week was designed the potential 1969 MINI. … What would it look like if it had come out in 1969, new?

"I thought of all the social things that were going on in the world. And what that 1969 MINI could have looked like. I updated it thinking not just about a '69 look, but with a '69 car based on what the world needed at that time.

"Then … the second week, I did the 1979 MINI. That changed because, you remember the Volvos in the '70s were all about safety and boxy … cars were getting really boring. So, I designed the 1979 MINI to reflect those values.

"In the third week, I did the '89 MINI and we were getting … to bring fun back to motoring and cars got to look a bit more wedgey and dynamic…

"And the last week, the fourth week, was the '99 MINI."

Fifteen designers were given the assignment: redesign the MINI for the next generation. The only solid parameters being the general length of a car and to modernize it for the twenty-first century.

"Build us a modern mousetrap," they were told (obviously not literally, and in the context of the MINI, probably a bit more apt than intended, but I digress).

Fourteen designers heard the challenge and set forth to make their mark on the new MINI. But Frank thought about it differently: he designed a fictional history of impact of the MINI on the world, to see where that evolution would have brought him.

"When you look at that '99 Mini, it was the great grandchild … of the original MINI; there was that DNA, a genetic link … [it was] bigger, faster, stronger, more intelligent than [its great grandfather], super, super improved version of him. Although

[you] just see the evolutionary link that you have with your great grandfather."

THEN AND NOW

Alec Issigonis had been given a list of very specific requirements when creating the original. The fifteen designers in 1995 were given only the length. Alec had to rethink the common approach to car design.

Fourteen other elite designers chosen by one of the top automotive companies in the world designed a car the way they knew how to design a car. They designed the car they wanted to exist that met the requirement they were given.

However, with Frank … innovation doesn't quite begin to describe his thought process. Where others attempted to make their own car to be called a MINI, Frank actually sought to bring Alec Issigonis' MINI to the future. His outside-the-box thinking was actually looking at what was in the box, where he started, making sure to be respectful of the history that was already there.

THE WHEEL WANTS TO BE REINVENTED (IT TOLD ME)

Small updates over thousands of years brought us the wheel we know today. The Tire Industry Association recognizes no less than thirty-one classes of tires, each consisting of numerous technologies and subtypes.

You could easily argue those are all just wheels; they are reinventions of the application, construction, and material. As of 2024, GM has announced it is introducing the next evolution of the wheel with a new tire system markedly different from anything we've seen before.

Even if you then take away all transportation, eliminating roller skates, roller blades, skateboards, bicycles, etc. … That leaves us with the water wheel, mills, gyroscopes, grain grinders, and so on. The wheel (and its central technology, the axle) has been applied in thousands of applications, variations, and designs.

Don't stop rethinking the wheel.

Marty: Hey, Doc, you're gonna have to back up; we don't have enough road to get to 88!
Doc Brown: Roads? Where we're going, we don't need roads.
—BACK TO THE FUTURE I AND II (1985 AND 1989)

CHAPTER TWELVE

STOP CRYING AND START THINKING

TL;DR—Frank Stephenson, designer of the new MINI, also designed the BMW x5 and Fiat 500 using a unique approach and innovative process to the problem. Excuses are just a pay-wall to progress. You can always find a way to accomplish the goal. We need to focus on what is needed, not what is asked for.

No problem can't be fixed. Only problems we are looking at wrong.

That does not always mean that we can get the solution we want, or that things can end well. But we can always, 100 percent of the time, find a solution if we look at an issue from every available angle.

I've heard it a lot throughout my career: "We don't have the money." "We can't do that this year." "There's just no way to do it." "It can't be done."

THESE ARE SILLY OBJECTIONS

They are excuses; they don't actually exist. These are "self-imposed" limitations from perceived obstacles.

Oftentimes, they are said in earnest. They are statements of genuinely believed limitations. I also know they are used to stop people from questioning an unrelated non-desire to get the project done. They are used as a paywall to progress.

Excuses are the rallying cry of the uninspired to enable the unmotivated to accept the unremarkable.

When we allow a limitation to end a line of thinking or a path to progress, we are allowing others to dictate what we can accomplish.

During the building of our studio at Glass River Media, one of the engineers came to me to say we wouldn't be meeting a deadline. I tend to be fairly laid back in most situations, but punctuality and deadlines remain a massive neurosis of mine.

I asked, "Okay, what seems to be the problem? Why can't it get done this week?"

They gave a list of five things that sounded like reasonable limitations and said them with such authority and confidence. I truly believed they were at a dead end. I don't like dead ends.

I TAGGED MYSELF IN

With the help of some of my team, we dug into the five things on the list, and we either fixed them or established solid workarounds in about ninety minutes. In fact, the workarounds and fixes were shockingly easy.

I went back to the engineer:

"Hey, great news, we fixed it. All of the problems you were having are gone, and we can make the deadline."

He frowned and looked at me, disappointed. That's when I figured it out. These weren't limitations; these were excuses to not have to meet the deadline.

They were "reasonable" excuses to hide the real reasons. The real reasons were equally reasonable: he wanted to take a day off, and the deadline was too aggressive for his tastes. We talked about it, I extended the deadline, and life moved on.

Missing the deadline? Not that big of a deal—we compensated.

Realizing that I couldn't trust my engineer to be straight with me? Actually damaging.

Excuses are the rallying cry of the uninspired to enable the unmotivated to accept the unremarkable.

Frequently, obstacles get in the way and feel insurmountable.

But we also often use things that seem hard to give us permission to quit.

DESIGN IT ON THE PLANE ...

As we just met Frank Stephenson, the designer chosen to redesign the MINI, in the last chapter, let's talk a bit more about the man who might as well be the real-life Tony Stark. He is a far more all-encompassing exemplar of a creative, and a designer to look up to in his ability to look at a situation from every possible angle.

When reaching out to people to interview for this book, I had three lists: friends and family to bounce ideas off and gather perspective from, industry insiders and experts to give me feedback and insights, and rock star exemplars who would be amazing but who I assumed would never take my call. Frank was on that last list. He took the call.

We spent over two hours on Skype one morning talking about everything from Maserati to Motocross. I already knew his designs were second to none, but I hadn't realized until that call just how inspirational this man truly is.

Frank Stephenson was born in Casablanca, Morocco, to an American father and Spanish mother. He speaks six languages, has traveled the world, has competition-winning Bernese mountain dogs, once rebuilt his Ducati from scratch after it decided to take ITSELF for a ride, and is the designer of some of the most iconic, groundbreaking, beautiful pieces of automotive engineering in our generation. With all due respect to Dos Equis, Frank Stephenson is actually the most interesting man in the world.

I have pages of notes and observations from our relatively brief conversation, but three stories I will tell the rest of my life. The first was that of the MINI. However, almost more incredible is the story directly before it in his career, that of the BMW X5.

BIRTH OF THE X5

BMW had never had an SUV. The car company with a long and varied history in engineering had been a staple in the smaller sports coupe and full-sized sedan, but until the 1990s when it acquired Land Rover, BMW had never ventured into the sports utility market. The company decided it was time to fix that.

For reasons that delve into the politics and economics of the automotive industry, and perhaps eager executives, the top brass at BMW wanted a full-size working model of the proposed SUV in six weeks. Which was possible, but only barely. The task would require a dedicated team, working eighteen-plus-hour days, seven days a week.

The problem was that prohibitive unions and legislation in Munich made that illegal. They were going to need to out-source to a country with more permissible labor laws.

Italy.

Chris Bangle, then head of design for BMW, came to Stephenson, one of his lead designers on a Friday, and said:

"Frank, you're going down to Turin on Sunday. You're starting to work on Monday, you're going to be at this small concept house ... and they're going to build an SUV for you, full-scale.

And you're going to come back in six weeks and present it to the engineering director."

Just one problem ... at the top of the list of a lot more problems with that plan.

Frank replied, "Okay, I go down there and I come back in six weeks with the SUV, full-size model—what's it look like?"

"That's up to you," Chris replied.

"What do you mean?" Frank was a bit incredulous. "Where do I start? You said I start Monday?!

"Chris, that only leaves me Saturday, or the rest of today, Friday, and Saturday to design a car. That's ridiculous. I'll need to pack, prepare to be gone, I can't just go. When do I do the design?"

"Well," Chris said, *"you'll have time on the flight."*

I checked: a flight from Munich to Turin is roughly two hours.

But, according to Frank, that is exactly what happened:

"I sat on the flight, and I sketched out on the paper I brought with me ... what a future BMW SUV could look like. ... Sunday afternoon, April of '94, with pieces of paper sketched out, a translator picks me up and takes me to the shop on the outskirts of Turin ...

"We arrive to this big door and these three old guys stand in their plaster-covered overalls smoking their little Italian cigarettes and drinking tiny espresso."

Frank looked at his translator, concerned; these were older men, so clearly there must be a mistake.

"I say to the translator, 'These guys are going to work seven days a week at least eighteen hours a day for six weeks? They're kind of old, for that intensity, aren't they?'"

To which the translator replied, "Don't you worry about these guys. They are the same three guys that built the Lamborghini Miura."

For those who are automotively uninitiated, the Lamborghini Miura is often considered "the Golden Chalice" of classic design. It was one of Lamborghini's first cars and the one that put them on the map.[95]

"Every designer put the Lamborghini Miura in their top three of the most beautiful cars in the world. And so back when they were in their late twenties, they built the Lamborghini Miura design. ... These are three guys that were building this model for me."

"I felt like I was in front of DaVinci."

---

95 "Original Influencer: The History of the Lamborghini Miura | Automobile Magazine - Automobile." 2019. Automobile.

And so they worked, as expected, for six weeks, essentially nonstop. With nothing more than experience and paper sketches, Frank Stephenson and the three sculptors of the Miura. No design overview, no approval process, just the instruction to go to Italy and come back with an SUV.

MUNICH, SIX WEEKS LATER

Standing with the engineering boss out on the viewing platform on top of the development center in Munich, the team waited to hear his thoughts. He took one clockwise lap around the car, paused, took one counterclockwise lap, and said, "Okay, that's it, we're going into production with it."

"And that was the first X5, great day, you feel like … you got slapped on the back and congratulated by the pope or something. But at the same time, it was like, 'Wow, you know, my gut paid off, because I couldn't design it in a logical way, just had to use my gut.'"

The success of the X5 segued almost directly to the MINI. Creating out of nothing the first SUV for a renowned luxury car brand, to updating one of the most iconic cars in the world … seems to constitute a pretty good chapter in Frank Stephenson's career.

THE NEXT CHAPTER:
GIVE THEM WHAT THEY NEED, NOT WHAT THEY ASK FOR.
But what happens when you create BMW's first SUV on scratch paper on a tray table on a two-hour flight with only six weeks to bring it to reality and then segue that success directly into reimagining one of Europe's most iconic cars?

People notice.

In July of 2002, Ferrari-Maserati appointed Frank its director of concept design and development. He was now working for arguably the most renowned and exotic luxury sports cars in the world. A force to be reckoned with and at the top of his game, he could do no wrong... and his boss called him in.

The president of Ferrari told Frank he was sending him to Fiat.

While Frank had nothing against the classic Italian family car, this move felt like a demotion. Frank lamented: what had he done wrong? How had he gone from Ferrari to Fiat? But the president assured him the reason was quite the contrary.

They didn't have anyone else they thought could do what needed to be done.

Fiat had a new man in charge, from outside the automotive industry. Frank met with him on Monday, and the new big boss laid out the would-be issue and new assignment:

"Look, I don't know much about cars … but I know about money. And if we don't have a new car in the market that is a worldwide success in ten months, we are going to tank. So, we need you to come up with a design and have it ready to go in ten months."

Frank was in disbelief. From the day a new car is conceived, designed, approved, and tested, the process takes, with relative certainty, five years. Japanese companies have managed to streamline the process down to three, and if you aren't too concerned with test drives and are willing to have your customer be your "dummy," you could potentially get the process down to eighteen months. But that really is the bare limit.

As Frank did with the X5, you can do a prototype in a few weeks, but a fully tested, legally approved vehicle takes years.

His response, "Yeah, you obviously aren't familiar with automotive development. It just literally does not happen … I'm sorry, I can't. It's impossible. I wish I could do it, but nobody's ever designed and developed a car in ten months; this would be an unheard-of form of witchcraft."

However, the orders were simple: "Well, that's your job."

"I went back to hotel and cried my eyes out, because I thought, 'You're going to fail on this one.'"

Not to be like a father ruining the movie, but this next part is my favorite part and the reason why Frank is a hero of mine.

Frank understood something that many people miss. What he'd been asked to do was not what they needed. He'd been asked to produce a car from scratch and have it in the market in ten months. That was out of the question. It isn't possible. But like our much-repeated mousetrap, that directive fell painfully short of adequately describing the goal.

"Every problem has a solution, it's just which angles you want to come at it from.

"Design and develop a new car and have it on the road in ten months: that was out of the question...

"Which, after I stopped crying, I started thinking."

The requirement to have a car on the market in ten months with high enough volume to sufficiently increase revenue— there might be a possibility.

To an executive who "didn't know much about cars" those concepts sounded a lot like the same thing. But fact of the matter is, they aren't.

Frank rallied and got to work; what he was going to need was a car that had already been tested, proven, and was road ready. Something he could add design to and get into production without needing additional engineering, certification, legislation, road tests, etc.

He needed a working Fiat that he could "Frank." (← not sure how he'll feel about being turned into a verb, but I'm going to go with it).

Enter the Fiat Panda. First hitting the roads in 1980, it was a small, no-frills, utilitarian vehicle designed for the purpose of getting people on the road at an affordable price point. It had been on the road for over twenty years. It wasn't much to look at, as it wasn't ever designed to be. But it would work as a platform.

Now for a bit of Fiat history. At roughly the same time as the UK was releasing the original MINI (1959), Fiat released the Fiat 500. Unlike the MINI, the 500 had left production in 1975. But in its day, this little vehicle was a sensation in Europe. Nicknamed "The Bambino," it sold over four million units in its under twenty-year history.[96]

"If I take the Panda, which we don't have to do any more testing on, we know that everything works, we just change clothes. We take the guy out of his work clothes, and we put him into a tuxedo."

They skinned the Panda—the car that Fiat had that worked the best. They removed "its hide" but kept the heart, soul, skeleton, and guts. A major facelift to revive the car and make it look like the modern version of the Fiat 500 as if it had been brought back today.

In 2007, the new Fiat 500 hit the streets. It has been a worldwide success.[97,98]

96   "History of an Icon: Fiat 500." 2020. ITALY Magazine.
97   Scottsdale, FIAT. 2020. "FIAT 500 | History of the FIAT 500 | In Scottsdale and Near Phoenix, AZ." Fiatusaofscottsdale.Com.
98   "History of the Fiat Panda - Part 2: First Series." 2018. DriveTribe.

The important takeaway of the Fiat story is this: Frank was called in to fix the problem. They told him his task. Just like the mousetrap, they set parameters they didn't need, due to an understanding they didn't have, and provided guidance that was actually impossible and counter to their actual goal.

Frank didn't give them what they asked for; he gave them what they needed. By using the pieces he already had, the design and history of the 500, and the working car of the Panda, he was able to save years of wasted time and millions of unnecessary dollars (or euros, as the case may be) to give them what they needed—his accomplishment wasn't invention.

Many people can design a fully functional car that is ready for the road. His accomplishment was in thinking about the problem from outside the direction he was given. He looked at the problem from outside the assigned parameters.

He made friends with the mouse.

THIS ISN'T NEW
The wheel's first use was in pottery.

It was rethought, and reapplied.

Rebranding, repurposing, reconfiguring, and rereleasing happens all the time.

Even "automotive facelifts"

were hardly invented by Mr. Stephenson.

But what doesn't happen often enough is removing the boundaries of the assignment, to get to the center of the requirement.

That part is what we need to focus on.

We are often given tasks from a place without all the information. We grumble and try to give them what they asked for. We need to focus far more on providing what they need.

"Perhaps a merger is a way to bring Bill's company into the twenty-first century, and perhaps it isn't.

"And perhaps cheating on your French philosopher's exam at the Groton School was an expedient way to get your diploma, and perhaps it wasn't.

"Be that as it may, Drew, a question can often be argued both ways."

—BRAD PITT AS JOE BLACK, MEET JOE BLACK, 1998

CHAPTER THIRTEEN

WE DON'T NEED NO EDUCATION

———

TL;DR—Schools were developed as a way to make good employees. Our education system doesn't encourage deviation. Charter schools sweep the nation. Summit Public Schools and Trellis approach the problems in education.

While I was giving a presentation on innovation and thought diversity to a group of educators, someone posed the following question to me:

"But don't we need to teach children the system before we teach them to look outside of it? Don't they need to know the rules in order to break them?"

The question filled me with delight. It was the most amazing question.

"No," I replied excitedly. "NO! We don't need to give them systems to chase out their originality before letting them solve the problem themselves."

"Let me give you an alternative approach," I excitedly professed …

Let's say you are an art teacher, and the curriculum says you are going to teach impressionism. On the first day, you pull up a picture of Van Gogh on the board, most likely his iconic self-portrait, and next to it you display Starry Night and his sunflowers.

The way our education system is currently set up, you'd then explain the medium he used, oils on canvas. You might go into the chemical breakdown of his particular type of oils or even the method of his canvas stretching.

His technique would be analyzed. His use of color dissected. His genius and process utterly (albeit incompletely) explained, with a makeshift structure attempting to teach would-be artists how to replicate the greats in a general paint-by-numbers application.

At the end of the lecture that would last forty minutes to four hours depending on the curriculum, the assignment would be issued: take a set amount of time and produce an image in the impressionist style like that of Vincent Van Gogh.

The students would then, as taught, follow the structure as explained, asking for assistance as they struggled, and would be redirected onto the path of the structure as needed.

At the end, some would have accomplished their assigned goal, while others would have "failed," had their inadequacies marked, and been given direction on how to correct them.

The structure in place, the rubric established, no room for personal experimentation. No space for failure.

BUT! What if, instead, you didn't do any of that?

What if you showed them the works of the impressionists, explained generally what the impressionist movement was, and gave them a table full of supplies with the only assignment being: figure it out.

A student would look at Monet's Water Lilies, not with the words of the teacher telling them how it was done, but with a critical eye and a goal of understanding and cracking the code. Some students would figure it out, others would fail. Not at a system explained to them, but they would succeed or fail at an approach of their own devising—how wonderful for both!

When the student approached the teacher with a canvas resembling a kindergarten finger painting … the educator would hand them a clean canvas and say, "Let's try that again."

After two or three attempts, deep analysis, and studying the "problem," a student of any form would be primed for information in a way that they weren't before. The neural pathways would be established, and a genuine question would exist, as opposed to an assignment with a predetermined goal.

BUT IT ISN'T JUST ART!

How amazing would the insights of the uninitiated be if instead of starting with the Pythagorean theorem or the established systems of old, we simply posed a quandary that said: how could we approach this?

Both Isaac Newton and Gottfried Wilhelm Leibniz nearly simultaneously developed calculus.[99] My favorite part of that fact is that, whereas the core math and results are in fact, the same, the processes, symbols, and general structure weren't.[100]

Both Leibniz and Newton developed the same system, but very much in their own way. For what it's worth, Isaac Newton is largely credited for being the father of calculus, but the form that was widely adopted and is currently taught is actually that of Leibniz (#TeamLeibniz).[101]

---

99 "Who Invented Calculus - Newton or Leibniz? Learn the History of Calculus." 2016. The Great Courses Daily.

100 "History and Applications - The Newton–Leibniz Controversy." 2020. Amsi.Org.Au.

101 17Th_Leibniz - The Story of Mathematics - A History of Mathematical Thought from Ancient Times to the Modern Day." 2020.

I have never been particularly adept at math, which is a polite way of saying that I have deeply struggled with math the entirety of my life.

However, for the most part, my hang-ups were in not understanding the problem. I didn't know why we were plugging numbers into this equation; I couldn't figure out why on earth it mattered, and I had no architecture in my brain for the information to stick to.

Just imagine if, instead of twelve years of teachers droning on about how other people solved things I didn't see as a problem, my instructors had instead given me a situation and asked me to navigate to the other side.

What if I was given the opportunity to find the problem, devise a system, a solution, a workaround? What if I was given the greatest of all opportunities: the chance to figure it out?

When I failed, when I came up short of the genius of Archimedes, Pythagoras, Newton, and Leibniz, wouldn't the solution now be more welcomed, firmly rooted in a problem I had my own understanding of?

BUT THAT ISN'T WHAT SCHOOLS ARE FOR

When you break out your tinfoil hat and join the land of loose tangential connections and bad Denny's coffee, an odd thing might occur to you: the inherent risk and near contradiction in having the same organization (be it a government, a church, a social club, or the Illuminati) control not just the administration of the society, but also what the society knows and how they approach an issue.

If you really dial up the tinfoil to the heavy duty industrial wrap, you might start to think the entire public school system was initiated by factory and mine towns as an employee benefit, but it was really to indoctrinate the children to be obedient eventual factory workers.

Despite that last hypothetical point being almost exactly what did happen and the genesis of standardized curriculums, you might start to realize the unbelievable propaganda engine you have when you control not just what someone knows, but what they think about it.[102,103,104]

But that is strictly if you want to be overly dramatic ... and people really seem to want to.

Our children are our future.

School and the welfare of our children are probably the fastest way to enrage the largest cross section of people. Parents take a wide array of perspectives and stances on their children, whether for them to be smarter, stronger, happier, more social,

102 "STOP STEALING DREAMS: Seth Godin at TEDxYouth@BFS."
    2020. YouTube.
103 Seth Godin "School Is Still Ruining Your Chances to Learn."
    2017. Medium.
104 Seth Godin "Education Needs to Be Inconvenient." 2018. Seth's Blog

less problematic, etc. Parents hand over an incredible amount of influence to an outside organization, in which they have essentially zero input when it comes to the curriculum.

For a majority of eighteen-year-olds, thirteen years of their lives have been spent in the public school system (or perhaps cynically stated, the formalized indoctrination of information by the same organization that governs, taxes, and legislates them).

"President Business is gonna end the world?!
But he's such a good guy!
And Octan, they make good stuff …
Music, dairy products, coffee, TV shows, surveillance systems,
all history books, voting machines.
Wait a minute?!"

—CHRIS PRATT AS EMMET, THE LEGO MOVIE, 2014

CONSPIRACY THEORIES ASIDE:
Public schools have been a blessing and benefit to millions of children since their original inception. But the school system in general has been under scrutiny for decades now. What is: science versus religious tradition? Standardized testing? Teacher-proof curricula? Common Core? Sex ed? Prayer in schools? Sexist dress codes? Zero tolerance policy? STEM versus arts? Is cheerleading a sport?

Controversy seems to drip from these institutions of "need-to-know."

OBLIGATORY CLICHED QUOTE

"Everyone is a genius. But if you judge a fish by its ability to climb a tree, it will live its whole life believing that it is stupid."[105]

~~ALBERT EINSTEIN~~

As we covered in "credit misfiled" and have seen with quotes by Theodore Roosevelt, Henry Ford, and Ralph Waldo Emerson, people's genius is often "borrowed" to advance someone's point artificially. To that end, we have no evidence that the great Albert Einstein had anything to do with the above statement, but however genuine the quote, it makes a solid point.

By developing a curriculum and system of education intended to overcome the variety of different cultures, lifestyles, and regional specific wisdoms, we created a different set of problems. For all the benefits of having a standard of learning, we created a standard of information, divvyed out in prescribed intervals, giving minimal allowances for individual learning styles, affinity for a subject, or relevance of it.

Our drive to track and monitor progress "required" us to make something we could measure. We needed benchmarks, so we created a "standard" for our children's education. A handy way to sort out the bright ones from the simple ones.

We established "the best way" for them to learn.

---

105 "Everybody Is a Genius. But If You Judge a Fish by Its Ability to Climb a Tree, It Will Live Its Whole Life Believing That It Is Stupid – Quote Investigator." 2020. Quoteinvestigator.Com.

We discerned "the best things" for them to learn.

We calculated "the best schedule" for optimized learning.

And the ridges and inconsistencies of young minds that are ill-matched to adhere to those prescribed standards are "corrected," medicated, or left behind.

STORY TIME

My oldest daughter as a toddler could and would get into anything. Her problem-solving skills were actually incredible. Her ability to outthink any obstacle set in front of her was astonishing. Not saying she is awaiting early admission to the Ivy League, but her mother and I were in awe of a young mind at work.

Even into kindergarten, she was bright, inquisitive, and experimental. The change didn't happen overnight, but by about second grade she started coming home telling us how "stupid" she was.

In the fourth grade, I was called in to have a meeting at her school.

I sat at a large table with her vice principal, her teacher, a social worker, a child psychologist, and her guidance counselor.

Then I had them, in very solemn but supportive tones, explain to me their concerns with her ongoing "failures."

I won't recount the whole meeting, but statements made included:

- "She asks too many questions and doesn't understand even when all the other kids do."
- "Other kids tease her because she doesn't understand."
- "She sometimes gets really frustrated and anxious when we have to move on."
- "Her test scores are below our school average, and we are an academically oriented school, who take our test scores and state ranking very seriously."

No amount of conversation with the school could get them to see my daughter as a person who needed a different approach, rather than a blotch on their testing record.

We homeschooled her the next year and took her to a different school the year after that. Things are better, but the damage is ongoing, because while the school and teachers are different, the rigid curriculum is the same.

Unfortunately for our circumstance, this solution was our only and best option.

But there has to be a better answer out there, somewhere, right?

ENTER THE CHARTER SCHOOL

Volumes of books have been written about the charter school. It tends to whip up a lot of controversy, rubs many education insiders the wrong way, and is said by its critics to be a fundamentally "bad idea."

Which by definition means I'm a big fan.

For those who aren't specifically aware of the rise of charter schools in the United States, here's an overview, as defined by the National Charter School Resource Center:

"A charter school is a public school that is independently run. It receives greater flexibility over operations in exchange for increased performance accountability. The school is established by a 'charter,' which is a performance contract describing key elements of the school. The charter contract describes things like the school's mission, instructional program, governance, personnel, finance, plans for student enrollment, and how all these are measured."[106]

Ray Budde first defined and conceptualized the concept of the charter school in 1974. He presented a paper titled "Education by Charter" to the Society for General Systems Research.[107]

As he would say in an interview many years later, Budde always had great interest in "the way things are organized"

106 NCSRC | National Charter School Resource Center."
    2020. Charterschoolcenter.Ed.Gov.
107 Budde, Ray. 1988. "Education By Charter: Restructuring School
    Districts. Key to Long-Term Continuing Improvement in American
    Education." Publication Sales, Regional Laboratory for Educational
    Improvement of the Northeast and Islands

and "how things work." After he wrote and presented his paper, he asked around.

"Does it make sense?!"

"Would a district be willing to give it a try?!"

His innovative reframing of the situation, redefining of a system, and reorganizing of "the way it works" were met with zero interest and a little bit of disdain … and his idea was shelved.

However, not terribly long after, in 1983, Ronald Reagan's National Commission on Excellence in Education released a report titled "A Nation at Risk: The Imperative for Educational Reform."

The report was snatched up by the media, because nothing sells a newspaper like children in danger. A report from the Carnegie Forum followed suit, and education reform became the new stump speech: "… think of the children … they are our future …"

In 1988, Budde unearthed his report from its fourteen-year tomb and had it published by the Northeast Regional Lab. Not wanting to miss the opportunity for this document to go around, he also dropped it in the mail to every address and potentially interested set of eyes he knew about, including 1600 Pennsylvania Ave, the then home of President George H.W. Bush.

It caught the attention of American Federation of Teachers, President Al Shanker. The story from here goes through many of the steps and pitfalls of any new endeavor, especially one involving any portion of the government.

Al Shanker, in fact, is often given a great deal, if not the line share, of credit for the invention of the charter school due to his championing through this process. His credit, remarkably due, was also misfiled.[108]

But in 1991, Minnesota passed a law that would allow for the opening of a charter school, and in 1992 the first one opened its doors.[109]

Neither Budde nor Shanker invented anything new here. They didn't create an education inception engine that downloads information directly into our brains. They didn't even strictly develop a specific method of teaching. Their "big idea" was to allow for new ideas.

Each charter would be granted based on the merits of that school's concept. Each institution, while needing to adhere to the same standardized test scores and accreditation, could teach the information in any way they saw fit.

"Here's all the rope you need."

---

108 Peterson, Paul. 2010. "No, Al Shanker Did Not Invent the Charter School - Education Next." Education Next.

109 Joy Schroeder 2004, "Ripples of Innovation: Charter Schooling in Minnesota, the nation's first charter school state" Progressive Policy Institute p. 24

This development is a monumental breakthrough. A government willing to allocate public funding toward new approaches?! Not just a grant, nor permission to write papers about it, but actual funding to operate a public school with negligible curriculum oversight? This concept truly is the very best bad idea.

This is exactly what I was saying at the top of the chapter. Here is an issue; figure it out.

I say with a genuine smile on my face:

Think of all the wonderful things that could go wrong?! Think about all the amazing things we could learn from that?

Of course, this funding with lack of oversight has led to abuse and scam artists over the last twenty-five-plus years. We have seen numerous controversies: schools closing mid-school year, misuse of funds, plagiarizing previous charter applications. Still smiling … what an unbelievably reasonable cost to pay toward the application of new approaches.

"If you build it, they will come."

—FIELD OF DREAMS, 1989

Minnesota was first in 1992, but California wasn't far behind. In 1993, it became the second state to open its doors to a new way of thinking about education.

The new law would allow for one hundred total charters in the state and no more than ten per district. San Carlos Charter Learning Center in San Mateo County has the distinction of being the very first.

SUMMIT PUBLIC SCHOOLS

"We believe that every child is capable of college and career success. Summit Public Schools is a leading network of public schools that prepares a diverse student population for success in a four-year college and to be thoughtful, contributing members of society."

"We founded our inaugural school, Summit Prep, in 2003. Today, we are proud to operate some of the best public schools in the country, serving diverse communities throughout California and Washington states."[110]

—SUMMIT PUBLIC SCHOOLS WEBSITE

Ten years later, the limitations to the number of charters had been removed, and charter schools were booming. Summit Prep opened its doors in the San Francisco Bay area, started by a group of parents of elementary school children looking for two things they couldn't seem to find in their available public options.

First, they wanted to know that the schools their children were attending were in fact high-quality schools, something they didn't feel they had.

---

110 "Summit Public Schools." 2020. Summitps.Org.

Second, they wanted their schools to reflect the diversity of the area in which they lived.

Adam Carter is the executive director for the Marshall Street Initiatives at Summit Public Schools, but perhaps more importantly, one of the first teachers in the program.

He was there for the development and drawing new edges on the changes they wanted to see in the system.

Adam told me that what started as a group of parents looking for solutions to issues they saw in their school district changed when they came upon the charter laws and the opportunities they represented.

After a series of community hearings, and what I can only imagine was an unpleasant amount of red tape, Summit Public Schools was formed. They had assembled their founding team, crafted their new approach, and gathered a student body that was truly diverse and an appropriate representation of the community it served.

The group's "new" approach is what really grabbed me about their story. Their first building wasn't a traditional school building. As such, it didn't have traditional classrooms. This difference did a lot to change the mentality, the expectations, and the perceived limitations:

Calling again on my art class example, charter schools weren't given a method and technique and held to a standard of making a school. They had a goal and a table of supplies to figure it out.

Adam's classroom he compared to a car dealership, as it was a long room with little glass cubicle-like partitions to the side.

"We were free from lots of constraints," he said, "so we could start with what the kids needed, and then built a school around them."

Their system didn't take long to take hold; in two years they were ranked among the top schools in California … and stayed there. The 2019 National Public School Ranking by the U.S. News World Report has Summit Preparatory Charter High school as the No. 3 school in the San Francisco metro area, the No. 17 school in California, the No. 39 Nationally for Charter Schools; Russo ranked No. 148 for all public schools in the United States.

If for some reason that number sounds high to you, please note that we have 132,853 public schools K through 12 in this country.[111]

Pretty amazing numbers for throwing out the traditional classroom and approaching the problem in a new way.

I can't say that the success of Summit Prep played a role in the near explosion of charter schools, but from 2003 to 2015,

---

111 "Summit Preparatory Charter High." 2019. U.S. News Report. Accessed Dec 09, 2019

the numbers of charters in both California and across the nation skyrocketed.

The National Alliance for Public Charter Schools reports that in the 2015–16 school year there were 1,234 charters serving approximately 581,100 students, representing 9.18 percent of the students of just California. Nationwide amounted to 6,855 total charter schools rising from 1,993 in the year 2000.

To compound the complexity of a situation critics already compare to the Wild West of education: the "first" charter school concept and the ongoing developing definition of charters and manifestations of it have morphed wildly across the practice.

As such, not all these schools are success stories. Some failed. Some failed catastrophically.

Not even Summit, with its amazing numbers and incredible numerical track record, is "all success stories."

The Summit model has some vocal critics. A number of early supporters left the organization as it grew, feeling that choices being made were antithetical to the original mission or impact.

But pushback is expected and acceptable when you're trying new things.

In 2015, in association with the Chan-Zuckerberg Initiative (yes, Mark Zuckerberg's philanthropy with his wife) Summit

Public Schools released a "personalized learning software system," called the Summit Learning Platform and piloted the program to nineteen schools across the country …[112]

Which grew to 380 schools by 2019.[113]

The Summit Learning Program, which is notably now a wholly distinct organization from Summit Public Schools and trying to offer all institutionalized learning for free to the greatest number of people possible.[114]

Even still, parents have "opted out" and "rebelled" against the Summit "Personalized Learning" system in Connecticut, Kentucky, Ohio, Pennsylvania, and Idaho.[115] Their complaints vary by situation, but a common thread is parents saying variations of "the system isn't right for their child."

Building a standard that will work for everyone everywhere seems almost impossible. Perhaps what works for one group of people, community, or set of circumstances can't be applied to the whole with standardized results … no, that can't be it.

---

112 "Why Do So Many Parents Opt Out of Summit Learning? | Elearninginside News." 2018. Elearninginside News.
113 "About Charter Schools | National Alliance for Public Charter Schools." 2020. National Alliance For Public Charter Schools.
114 "Summit Learning Is Spreading with Little Evidence of Success." 2019. Chalkbeat.
115 "Why Do So Many Parents Opt Out of Summit Learning? | Elearninginside News." 2018. Elearninginside News.

Critics of charter schools point at these as proof that the concept is a failed idea that should be put to rest. And in many areas, they are succeeding. At the time of writing, the charter laws are under review in many states and districts across the country, with groups calling for reform or removal of the practice.[116]

Just remember, kids:

> ## "If at first you don't succeed, you're a failure who should have never tried to do something in the first place."

(I'm going to have that needlepointed on a pillow.)

PERHAPS PEDANTIC, PERHAPS HYPOCRITICAL

It wouldn't be unfair to say that creating a new school system is, in fact, "building a better mousetrap," and it wouldn't be entirely untrue.

However, the core "better mousetrap" represented by charter schools is to allow them the freedom to do things that couldn't be done in the structure of the original "mousetrap."

They didn't aim to fix education with radical new technology, or downloadable brain upgrade software. They wanted the freedom to make the curriculum about the individual

---

116 Key Facts About Charter Schools." 2020. In-Perspective.Org.

students, and the established public school charter laws allowed them to do that.

CONCLUSIONARY MUSING

If the history of thinking is an important backdrop to understanding innovation and creativity, our current education system is a solid set piece to understand as well.

Differing opinions, regions, political parties, and agendas at large make "education" about a lot of things other than, well … "education." Are schools intended to be a hub of essential knowledge? Ambition generators? Advanced institutionalized daycare? I know people who would firmly stand behind each of those options.

Instead of teaching our future generations a strict structure of solving yesterday's problems, why not prepare them to better understand the problem? Instead of requiring a strict adherence to a structure, why not first issue those trying to learn something with the only two things we are ever really given by the world:

A DEADLINE AND A DELIVERABLE.

MOTIVATION

We must eat. We must eat at specific intervals.
Deadline: Today.
Deliverable: Food.
Figure it out.

We need shelter; we need protection from the elements.
Deadline: Before nightfall.
Deliverable: Walls and roof.
Figure it out.

Math Homework:
We need to understand geometry for the purposes of xyz.
Deadline: Tomorrow for class.
Deliverable: How tall would a ladder need to be to reach the fifth floor of a building leaning from at least a thirty-degree angle?

You and I both know that a formula exists for that.

Imagine how amazing it would have been if you were assigned the task of figuring that out, before you knew that.

At the end of the day, the biggest impediment to "making friends with the mouse" is largely this:
We aren't teaching or training people to try.

CHAPTER FOURTEEN

G.I. BEANS AND
G.I. GRAVY, GEE I WISH
I'D JOINED THE NAVY

TL;DR—The military sees the need to innovate. Army Futures Command and 75th Innovation Command are instituted to win tomorrow's wars. MG Boe Young requires beanbag chairs to make a point of innovation.

In the terms of general oxymorons and humorous contradictions, among those who have served in the Armed Forces, "Military Intelligence" stands as a noted example. It's often a poke at the general bloated bureaucracy that reigns as the prevailing driver of everything within the Department of Defense.

Very few organizational types have been annotated in the annuls of history with a longer run than military. It seems that no sooner did man emerge from caves and learn to draw on walls than they started telling the tales of epic battles and how to beat your enemy in the field of combat.

Similarly, very few technological innovations throughout recorded history haven't quickly, after their introduction, been weaponized or incorporated into a warfighter mentality. Flight, photography, internal combustion, giant beanbag chairs.

Wait ... what did Kirk just say? Beanbag chairs? What do beanbag chairs have to do with "warfighter mentality"?

THE ARMY LOOKS TO BUILD A BETTER MOUSETRAP

In 2018, during an initiative to increase production and shorten the innovation cycle within the military, the Department of Defense saw the creation of two new major change engines. In the active "regular" Army, it was the Army Futures Command, and in the Army Reserve, the 75th Innovation Command (although at the time of this writing, the name is under potential change review).

Each would have a different scope and purpose with the same general mission: to prepare our troops and the United States to defend against and defeat our enemies in TOMORROW's wars.[117,118]

---

117   Judson, Jen, and Jen Judson. 2019. "Army Futures Command Is Ready
        For Prime Time." Defense News.
118   "75Th Innovation CMD." 2020. Usar.Army.Mil.

YES, KIRK, VERY NICE ... BUT THE BEANBAG CHAIRS, WHAT WERE YOU SAYING ABOUT THE BEANBAG CHAIRS!?!

The US military has a major infrastructure built around scenario-based training. Every school, division, branch, and major command of the US military is focused heavily around playing and replaying scenarios. Some obvious education benefit accompanies this, but it's by definition training in how to fight yesterday's wars, or at best, the wars we see as a current potential.

No significant intent nor engine in the military has been enacted to teach soldiers or leaders to predict the problem, analyze the data, react to insights, and avoid situations. In fact, any real "problems" identified by the military are often quickly outsourced. And training soldiers to think? No, in many ways, the approach is actually a bit the opposite.

THE OODA LOOP: A RECURSIVE PROBLEM

A cornerstone of leadership taught in the Army is called "The OODA loop," which stands for Observe, Orient, Decide, Act (repeat). This method isn't bad guidance and can be a useful tool, but it is by definition reactionary, as it requires one to first observe. It positions all leadership to wait to react to observations before they can orient and make decisions.

So, what is the first thing you do when you are heading an initiative with the specific purpose of innovation, disruption, and change within the Army, an organization that is not only massive, but hemmed in by multiple levels of government and policy, including its own?

What if, above all else, that organization is built on a structure of traditions from an era when a flag, trumpet, and drum were the most effective form of battlefield communication?

YOU HIRE SOMEONE WHO DOESN'T LOOK AT STRUCTURE THE SAME WAY

We first met Major General James "Boe" Young in Chapter 10 and heard of his ability and willingness to throw out traditional structure and rank. MG Young had been asked to extend his service as the commanding general of the 75th TRAINING Command to lead the change into innovation. The Army needed an outside-the-box thinker, and MG Young had shown himself to be just that.

This fact might seem obvious—in fact, it might seem silly to even mention—but lots of people don't seem to understand something that is foundationally true:

IF YOU WANT SOMETHING TO CHANGE, YOU ARE GOING TO NEED TO CHANGE SOMETHING.

I have experienced a great many leaders throughout my career who didn't grasp this notion. They wrote a beautiful new mission statement, gave a rousing speech about a new plan of action, pointed toward the horizon (metaphorically), and encouraged the team to the future. But changed nothing.

They would get confused and frustrated; they'd emphasize their new vision in emails, and manifestos. Have events and team-building activities talking about the new quest, then functionally change nothing and watch to see what would happen. Nothing.

If you want your organization, team, product, output, ANYTHING to change, you have to change something. It sounds crazy, I know. However, doing so is also not always easy. Especially in the military, an old organization, steeped in history with a rigid adherence to a "way things are done."

Regulations exist that literally spell out how almost everything is done. They are not just passing policies, but essentially military law, written by our progenitors toward solving all issues of the future. It is a remarkably inefficient and fairly nonsensical paradigm. But MG Young and his team were set to make a dent in that. They knew matters needed to change, but first they wanted to see how the other half lived.

MG Young and his staff set out to tour technology firms, thought leadership consultancies, think tanks, and every other innovation hub that would have them. They toured Google, MIT, and the Duke Robotics Lab. They visited countless firms with the new era, Silicon Valley, jeans-and-sneakers vibe. Trying to find the common thread that connected them. Looking to identify a way of signaling the troops in the 75th that in fact something different was going on there.

In one such firm, MG Young noticed a large, comfortable-looking beanbag chair. Doing what we all would do (or at least think of doing), he fell down into it. This piece of furniture wasn't something you saw in a corporate setting very often, a giant beanbag chair. It certainly wasn't something you ever saw in a military setting. It might be perfect.

"Part of the cultural transformation would ... include a physical transformation of the workspace ... and some were somewhat easy to do. But other things were not as easy to do. "

—MG JAMES "BOE" YOUNG

At the same time, one of MG Young's working group similarly suggested a redesign of the physical appearance of the headquarters. The general approved and added to the list of requisite changes beanbag chairs. The new 75th Innovation Command would require beanbag chairs.

The budget for the transformation from Training Command to Innovation Command wasn't prohibitive nor small; resources to accomplish the mission were readily available. This new initiative had the support of the "higher-ups," and MG Young had a lot of latitude to play with.

But beanbag chairs seemed to be a bridge too far

Over the course of generations of military regulations, processes, and procedures, certain protections had been put into place.

To vastly oversimplify, if a specific military code wasn't attached to the utility of an item, it had not been deemed necessary, and therefore the military didn't have a mechanism by which to buy it.

Explanation: Every unit and type of unit has what is called its Military Table of Equipment or MTOE (pronounced M-Toe). This table has everything you need to succeed, from computers and desks to, if applicable, an Apache attack helicopter, a Striker assault vehicle, or Xerox copy machine. The MTOE is the recipe of all the elements to make your unit function. If it isn't on the MTOE, you can't have it.

But this fact shouldn't be a problem, right? Surely some code somewhere would allow for some discretionary spending. Surely this new initiative of innovation couldn't be halted so soon into the process by something so ludicrous as standard dorm room furniture.

But as it turns out, it could

The general staff all waited for the "joke" of the beanbag chairs to fade away, but MG Young continued to harp on it. Staffers would give reasons or regulations why the beanbag chairs couldn't be purchased, and with each excuse the general challenged, "We have to look at the problem differently."

"People didn't understand what the logic of this beanbag chair was or what we are talking about here. But the beanbag chair stood for something more than just a place to sit. It's time for a physical manifestation of how we're going to change the culture."

—MG YOUNG

One afternoon, while on the phone with the legal team for the whole of the Army Reserve at USARC headquarters regarding an unrelated issue, MG Young joked that this issue was becoming "more complicated than beanbag chairs." Then the USARC legal team informed him that they, at the top of all things "Army Doctrine," had already been informed and notified about the "beanbag chair issue."

To put that in schoolyard speak, someone had tattled to the lawyers.

If you were to go into the 75th Innovation Command headquarters today, in Houston, Texas, and make your way back to the command suite, you'd see them. Two beanbag chairs. Not like the big comfortable ones he saw in the Silicon Valley incubator. More of the Ikea dorm room variety. But they are there. The symbol of change.

This story may seem like a trumped-up tale of something inconsequential. But it symbolizes both the need for systemic innovation and cautions against rules so stringent they prevent the free flow of leadership.

Military regulation required "building" + "better" + "mousetrap" = "innovation." It had gone so far as to have regulations that prevented you from doing anything else. But MG Young didn't want a mousetrap, he was trying to release the Kreative held hostage by protocol—he intended to make friends with the mouse.

INNOVATION, INTELLIGENCE, AND INFLUENCE

In 2017, the 75th Training Command transitioned to the 75th Innovation Command, and MG Young was left to figure out what exactly that meant. He put away the rank structure for beanbag chairs. He led by challenging assumptions. He didn't want to see the limitations of regulations that didn't apply, nor the traditions that get in the way of progress. He wanted to change something, by changing something.

At the time of printing in 2020, with the government moving at the speed of government, we can't yet tell what effects the 75th Innovation Command (or whatever it will be called) has had or will have. But the structure set up by (now retired) MG Young is still there. Still working to break the OODA loop of reactionary leadership. Getting creative to face tomorrows threats.

They are at least trying to make friends with the mouse.

CHAPTER FIFTEEN

GREY MATTER, GREY AREA, AND GREY POUPON

———

TL;DR—Steve Jobs and Bill Gates were innovators, but their real accomplishments aren't readily discussed. When we know what tomorrow looks like, we shouldn't spend any more time on yesterday.

Prom night is fraught with cultural quips and associations, some of them positive, some negative. Corsages, rented tuxes, bad DJs, spiked punch, the list goes on. For many, prom is a rite of passage, while for others, prom night is a drab obligation, and some don't even bother.

My prom was a train wreck, but that story is long and unrelated. This first part, however, is relevant.

I wanted to swing for the fences and make an impression. I didn't just rent "a tux." I procured an epic three-piece amalgamation of bad '90s styling and youthful indiscretion. I didn't make reservations at some classy place for dinner, nor one of the many "events" sponsored for prom.

Nope, I took my date to the Rainforest Cafe (if you are unfamiliar, the Rainforest Cafe is a novelty themed restaurant that had a big swing in the '90s. With animatronic wild animals, giant fake trees, a massive aquarium, and a flashy thunderstorm every half hour. Seventeen-year-old Kirk thought he was so cool).

As for transportation, I knew that was the crux of the perfect evening. Everyone rented a "limo," and soon, whether it was white, black, a cadi, or a Lincoln, a town car or a Hummer, they all start to look the same.

But for me? Not gonna work. I rented a 1957 S1 Series Bentley with an English chauffeur in traditional boots, bloused pants, a double-breasted jacket with two shiny rows of brass buttons, and a jaunty cap. He arrived in my cul-de-sac and my heart leapt.

I approached the pearl-white beacon of automotive excellence and Jan (my driver) opened the door. As I went to climb in, he stopped me and expressed:

"Sir, as I know this is your prom and a very special evening, I made a stop on your behalf on my way over, I hope you don't mind."

He then reached into the car and produced for me a classic bottle of Grey Poupon.[119] It was truly the most epic moment.

Grey Poupon mustard is fairly well-known for its tongue-in-cheek mockery of itself through its long-running commercial campaign.

"Pardon me, do you have any Grey Poupon?"

"But of course."[120]

However, what less people know is the significance Grey Poupon actually had on the world.

It would be inaccurate to say that Maurice Grey "invented Dijon mustard." He didn't. Mustard seeds had been being ground as spice all over the world for centuries, and the chefs of Dijon France had been adding white wine and vinegar to create rich "Dijon mustards" for over a hundred years.

But it was a fairly manual process. The grinding, straining, sifting, and processing it took to produce a desirable mustard took a master's touch. Sixteen kilograms per day was all any one operation could produce and maintain any degree of quality.[121]

---

119 If for some reason you don't understand this joke, or why this is significant, please Google "Grey Poupon Commercial" … go ahead … I'll wait … good, now we're all on the same page.

120 Grey Poupon - Train (1984, USA). The Hall of Advertising (Commercial). November 16, 2015. Retrieved August 16, 2019.

121 "The History of Dijon Mustard." 2020. Kitchenproject.Com.

But in 1855, Maurice Grey developed a machine that greatly streamlined the process, making what was a multistep endeavor much simpler.[122] The result could produce fifty kilograms in a day. A partnership and financial backing of another mustard maker, Auguste Poupon, gave production and distribution a kick and put Grey Poupon mustard on dinner tables all over the world.

Their invention, born of the necessity to simplify the production, which involved a clunky and detailed process, into something more automated and faster, took their product (which I'm sure was arguably inferior to other hand-ground mustards of the time) and brought a new flavor palate all over the world.

Deli mustard, brown mustard, modern Dijon mustard, all the grandchildren of this invention. Grey Poupon made it happen.

But if "necessity is the mother of invention," well, then innovation is the mother of all "grey areas." Because frankly, what are "innovations" exactly? A few big ones that very few people question—the light bulb, the telephone, the airplane! Yeah! Those! But those aren't innovations, but rather inventions, and even they are hugely debated. If we take a closer look, even those have controversies and questions surrounding their ideas, implementations, timelines, and credits.

Alexander Graham Bell is the father of the telephone with his storied first words: "Mr. Watson—come here—I want to see you." However, that story as well is far from clear-cut. In

---

122 "The Condiment Mustard's History." 2020. The Spruce Eats.

Italy, the "inventor" of the telephone is recognized as Antonio Meucci. And Elisha Gray filed his patent for his talking telegraph on the same day as Bell, even with some controversy on who submitted it first.[123]

As we mentioned in "Credit Misfiled," Thomas Edison is credited with the "invention" of the lightbulb in 1880, but many working prototypes and earlier iterations of the technology were developed by Alessandro Volta, Humphry Davy, Warren de la Rue, William Staite, and Joseph Swan as far back as 1800.[124]

This narrative alone leads to controversies, as patent filings, timing, theft of concepts, etc. were scrutinized heavily and many believe not judged accurately. Edison held 1,084 patents, none that I can find that were actually unique nor initially developed by him.

Even the famous and storied invention of the airplane by Orville and Wilbur Wright, with their first powered manned flight in Kitty Hawk, North Carolina, is challenged by Brazil, which claims its own Alberto Santos-Dumont is the true pioneer of aviation.[125]

The controversies all stem from the murky grey waters of "originality" and "credit."

---

123 "Who Is Credited with Inventing the Telephone?" 2020. The Library of Congress.
124 McFadden, Christopher, Trevor English, and Trevor English. 2019. "Was Thomas Edison Really the Inventor of the Light Bulb?" Interestingengineering.Com.
125 "History Faceoff: Who Was First in Flight?" 2020. HISTORY.

Three masters of their craft all approach three adjacent sides of a beautiful skyscraper, the first of its kind, a record-breaking building that tickles the heavens. All three men stand with their families pointing up to the structure and say, "There it is, MY building. I BUILT THAT!"

The first man is a welder. He spent 2.5 years of his life climbing the steel, masterfully fitting all the joints and welding together the skeleton that gave structure to the dream.

The second man is the construction foreman. Over three million man-hours went into building this work of art. It took logistical nuance of supply line, budgets, schedules, materials, safety requirements etc. in a symphonic amalgamation like the most technical of ballets. He provided the nervous system, the life, the means, the purpose to this building. In addition to the body that his workers toiled to assemble, he brought to the building life, movement, energy, and action.

The third man is the architect. He visited the job site often, three to five times per week. He watched the progress from the office of his firm across town. He watched as "his building" erupted into the skyline. This is his signature on the world: it's more than just metal and glass—it's his soul.

All three men stand on the corner and tell their families about the building they built. Each appreciates the credit allotted within their contribution. Are any of the men wrong? Do any of them not deserve credit for building the building? Are any lying or being deceptive? No. Because credit is a muddled, semi-subjective conversation.

Credit delves into fame, notoriety, politics, chicken versus egg nauseating hypotheticals. However, the fact of the matter is: all fragments contribute. Does the architect have the skills to have completed the building himself? The design elements he employed—did he originate them, or were they classic elements inspired by something?

The welder, did he teach himself all he knew? Can't we assume that many of the techniques that drove him to be the main welder on a large project were contributed by outside sources?

Same with the foreman. His skills were not spontaneous; his preparation involved memories of diverse projects, lessons learned, pitfalls to avoid. He can find memories of unrelated success and find ways to apply them to creative new solutions.

But then we have bickering over which fragment is the prettiest, whose contribution the worthiest. Like the story of Sir Isaac Newton and Gottfried Wilhelm Leibniz independently developing calculus practically simultaneously several hundred miles from each other. Both men innovators regardless of credit (#TeamLeibniz).

We are within this grey area as we find ourselves discussing the "inventors" of the personal home computer. Two men whose contributions undoubtably changed the world: Bill Gates and Steve Jobs.

I see you rolling your eyes, and I'm with you. With no small degree of apprehension, I include Apple and Microsoft in this book, not because they don't qualify, but because they are the obvious, overused examples.

Bill Gates' general nerdy demeanor and Steve Jobs' black turtleneck and unshaved face are a part of our cultural codex, just as Michael Jordan is, whether or not you know anything about basketball, like David Beckham for soccer (the real football), or Wayne Gretzky for hockey.

However, carefully worded stories crafted by PR people are rarely rich in value. The stories told of Gates and Jobs are legendary, but so oversimplified and even dramatically inaccurate that they don't paint the "right" picture of why these men mattered.

The stories that show me the true guts of Microsoft and Apple lie in their thought leadership, not their technology or near global hegemony.

"Knowing is better than wondering, waking is better than sleeping, and even the biggest failure, even the worst, beats the hell out of never trying."

—ELLEN POMPEO AS MEREDITH GREY, GREY'S ANATOMY

GETTING THE JOBS DONE (← THIS PUN IS TERRIBLE)

Steve Jobs tells this story in a Stanford commencement address in 2005,[126] which circulated the internet so you may already know it …

---

126 "Steve Jobs Stanford Commencement Speech 2005." 2020. YouTube.

It starts when Steve Jobs quit Reed College after only one semester. He felt he was wasting his parents' hard-earned savings on what felt like an aimless path. So, with a free spirt, focused on frugality, he dropped all his courses.

This move gave him the time for the spiritual journey he wanted. A time to reflect on himself.

He took this time for mindfulness and deep introspection and studied far-reaching and diverse subjects. Including, of all things, calligraphy.

Reed College had a noted calligraphy program instructed by a former Trappist monk named Robert Palladino.[127] Attracted to the design and artistry, Jobs dropped in on the course and learned about type facing and serif and sans serif fonts. He studied scripts, block types, line and other styles. He loved the simplicity and intricacy. The topic helped provide a sense of simple design and beauty at a time when he was feeling void of any specific direction.

We all have stories like this. The thing we do to distract ourselves from being ourselves. The hobbies, pastimes, vices, or passions we use to clear our head. At the time, calligraphy was Steve's, and this point is where it could have ended. But instead, ten years later, this story and memory became relevant for Steve Jobs, who with Apple was creating the first graphical user interface for a home computer.

---

127 "The Only Reason the Mac Looks Like It Does Is Because Steve Jobs Dropped in on a Course Taught by This Former Monk." 2020. Business Insider

To that point, there were typewriters and early rudimentary word processors, which had one thing in common—clunky, often misaligned, immovable typefaces. That wasn't going to work for Jobs, who at his core needed things to express function in every facet of their design.

Something that "just got the job done" was never going to be enough. This class had instilled in him a love of beautiful type, the elegance and the history of fonts. He insisted and integrated font choices, sizes, bolds, and italics into his visual operating system.

Of the decision, Jobs recounted:

"It was the first computer with beautiful typography. If I had never dropped in on that single course in college, the Mac would have never had multiple typefaces or proportionally spaced fonts."

Steve Jobs used an experience, a misaligned memory, to innovate. He took calligraphy, a dying skill of a foregone era, taught by a former Trappist monk, and incorporated it into the next generation of computer technology.

Then, as the story goes, Microsoft "stole everything" from Apple, and the computer I am typing on now has 2,500 fonts. Innovation!

But that is far from the only example of Jobs not looking at the problem the same as everyone else. His frame of reference in general seemed to be a bit different.

Amit Chaudhary, a former Apple employee from the era of the first iPod development, relayed probably my favorite story of its creation:

As it is told, the engineering team brought Jobs the prototype for his review and approval. He scrupulously weighed the device and held it in his hands and examined it closely. Then he definitively rejected it:

"Make it smaller."

The team of engineers at Apple, and the whole of Silicon Valley for that matter, tend to be near the top of the game. We can assume this cohort of designers was no exception to that general standard. They explained that to make even this prototype they had to "reinvent inventing" (a phrase I'm particularly fond of) and that making it smaller was just not possible. This size was as compact as the components were capable of being.

Jobs reweighed the device in his hands, stood quietly, considering, then dropped the fledgling prototype in the large fish aquarium in the office. As the device settled into the sediment at the bottom, bubbles streamed from the seams and ports of the device and rose to the top.

"Those are air bubbles," he responded. "That means there's space in there. Make it smaller."

I've heard this story used as proof of Jobs' lack of bedside manner and social skills. I've also heard it used to "define" his technological innovation. It isn't really about either of those.[128]

In fact, it's a remarkably poor example of both. No, this anecdote is about using the most unconventional device imaginable, a fish tank, to measure the density and volume of a piece of leading-edge tech.

While being asked to build a smaller, tighter mousetrap, the best mousetrap designers in the world explained they'd hit their limit.

They were engineering masters (as you would have had to be during that era in Silicon Valley). They understood their expertise perfectly.

But for Steve, a memory, misaligned. A piece of common knowledge applied in a remarkably uncommon way. I can't say I know how Steve learned about bubbles floating. I'm sure it isn't a recorded story or tied to anything significant. However, we can safely assume that the memory did not originate in a tutorial to find empty space by volume. In a building full of the world's leading engineers and tools, a bucket of water was his key.

"Think Different," in all of its atrocious grammar, became the mantra and slogan of Apple. Their computers are great,

128 "Why Steve Jobs Drowned the First iPod Prototype | Cult of Mac." 2014. Cult of Mac.

but not technological leaders. Their design is great, but not earth-shattering or original. The near legendary rivalry of Jobs versus Gates is misunderstood. The whole matter was never truly about the computer; it was about disrupting the status quo and accelerating progress.

AN ENEMY AT THE GATES (← THIS PUN IS WORSE)

Like Edison, Ford, and Jobs, Bill Gates undeniably changed the world. But also, like Edison, people often misattribute how. To really understand his genius, you need to look past the glitter of flashing lights, examine the miles of microprocessors and copper coils, and inspect, of all things, his administrative policies (this is the chapter to help with insomnia, but stick with me).

In the late '90s, Microsoft was in full swing and expanding. It was hiring eighty-five people on average per week to accommodate the constant shifting of the marketplace and overall upgrade cycle of technology.

Think about how mundane filling out new hire paperwork is. Now imagine doing it before computers were a standard integration into the office space, and pretend the internet barely exists. Forms being filled out in triplicate was still a practiced methodology. HR people are often the busiest at a company. Payroll, leave, new hires, terminations—the job is very big. Now remove the internet and computers having any function beyond a word processor glued to a graphing calculator. And again, eighty-five new hires per week.

Microsoft had over 1,000 different individual forms to handle the internal administration of personnel. They printed an average 350,000 pages of sales reports each year.[129]

Microsoft, a booming technology company, wasn't embracing technology. Computers were finding more applications in American life, but we weren't there yet. The system wasn't in place. We can't force a change that people aren't ready for.

We have to work within the current system, right?

As it turns out, no

Over the course of two years, Bill Gates made the application process at Microsoft very nearly 100 percent online/email-based. He instituted systems that onboarded employees from their new-hire paperwork all the way to ordering paperclips for their new desk organizer a digital system. This change allowed for greater accuracy, greater efficiency, massive cost savings, and an overall reduction from 1,000 plus paper forms in 1995 to fewer than sixty in 1997.[130]

Among other things, this move made the data trackable, the order easily repeatable, and information overall more accessible.

---

129 Bill Gates, "Business @ The Speed of Thought" 1999,
     p.42 Management Paradise
130 Bill Gates, "Business @ The Speed of Thought" 1999,
     p.49 Management Paradise

But the true thought innovation from that era was best displayed in the pushback, and Gates' answer to it.

Not just internal to his own company, but with mass inclusion and introduction of Windows to major systems around the world. People were having a problem adopting, adapting, and responding to the technology cycle.

Mr. Gates was asked to come to speak to the board of a client in the European financial market who was actively incorporating the Microsoft platform. These were very "experienced" businesspeople (read: old). They didn't necessarily object to the concept of change, but the timeframe, necessity, and full integration required were causing some concerns.

In his 1999 book Business @ The Speed of Thought[131] he outlines the situation in more detail, but this is my core takeaway

He asked them:

"Do you believe that in the future people at work will use computers every day for most of their jobs?"

In the late '90s this scenario was hardly a reality for many workplaces.

"Do you believe that today's paperwork will be replaced by more efficient digital processes?"

---

131   Bill Gates, "Business @ The Speed of Thought" 1999, p.60-64 Management Paradise

We had been using paper to communicate for most of recorded history. The thought that this time might be a new era was a change of thinking for many.

"Do you believe that one day most homes will have computers?"

At this time, home computers were far from standard, and mostly only in upper-middle-class homes and above.

"One day, will computers be as common in homes as telephones or TVs?

This idea was NOT a foregone conclusion at the time.

"Do you believe that one day most businesses and most homes will have high-speed connections to the World Wide Web?"

Also not an assumption people were widely making (yet).

"Do you believe e-mail will become as common a method of communication among people in business and homes as the telephone or paper mail is today?"

Catching the theme yet? These weren't breakthrough technological advances. Bill Gates was asking remarkably intelligent, successful businesspeople to think outside their immediate frame of reference to reconsider technology they already had access to and understood. These questions were asking them to change the way they thought, not necessarily change what they did (yet).

But the questions didn't stop there:

"Do you believe that most information will start arriving in digital form?"

"Do you think your bills will arrive electronically?"

"Do you think digital equipment will become common?"

And then, most importantly:

"When do you think it is going to happen?"

The European men agreed that they believed all were coming, probably in only a few more years. They saw the writing on the wall. The difficult part was acting on it.

Gates told his clients to prepare themselves for three things:

1. Most of the contact between business and customers, business and business, and people and government will become digital and self-service.
2. Customer service will become the primary way of adding value in every business. Human involvement in service will shift from routine, low-value tasks to high-value personal service to the customer.
3. Companies will use a digital nervous system to regularly adapt their internal business processes to an environment that constantly changes because of customer needs and competition.

Reading this in 2020 (or beyond), these points seem obvious. Gates' book was written in 1999, and this conversation happened sometime in 1996 or 1997.

"To prepare for that change," Gates told them, "you need to make digital information flow everywhere in your organization."

This approach was a mental shift. The technological infrastructure of what he was asking for is actually a large distraction from the true innovation lost in this story for many. What he was asking was for successful, experienced titans in their field to change everything about the industry they understood and prepare for one they didn't.

INCREDIBLY UNCREDITED

Bill Gates is far from uncredited for his contributions to society. However, as I've read about him, I believe we herald him very much for all the wrong things. Gates said things that were absolutely on par with early-era sci-fi writers—evoking emotions and responses with promises of technology that was decades from reality, and saying it with an eye toward complete integration.

I don't know what memories he was using. Maybe they were that of Buck Rogers and Flash Gordon, but Gates knew he could integrate a new world of tech that had not been invented yet.

Windows is an operating system and Microsoft is a large successful tech company ... yes, agreed, noted.

Yet, weirdly enough, obfuscated by all this success is Bill Gates' real genius: he saw opportunities inside of problems.

True innovation isn't in the technology (even in this case where it actually was). Innovation is in understanding what the technology was doing and where it was going, along with implementing what you could when you could to be ahead of the market when it got there. The brilliance of Gates was adopting a mind frame that allowed for future thinking:

If we know tomorrow's solution, why would we spend more time or money on today's?

As discussed in the opening anecdotes of this chapter, credit is political, a grey area, and inconsequential. Did Steve Jobs or Bill Gates "invent" the modern computer? No, not really. Did they contribute? Sure, depending on what you mean by "invent." Where Gates and Jobs dominated was not in their inventions, not in their tech, but in their ability to wantonly disregard the status quo. Cast off the assumed present and adopt the potential future.

CHANGE IS THE ONLY CONSTANT

Outside of death and taxes, change is the only thing we can count on. We can't expect things to be comfortable or consistent. We're dealing with too many moving pieces, and the more control you have of your environment, the more you attempt to thwart inevitable change, the more catastrophic the change will be.

Expect change, welcome change, embrace change.

"Resistance is futile."

—THE BORG, STAR TREK

PART THREE

RELEASE THE KREATIVE

CHAPTER SIXTEEN

LET'S GET KRAKEN

———

TL;DR—The Kraken is a sea monster that is an embodiment of how vast and deep the ocean is, and how little we know about it. You are an ocean, deeper, scarier, and more interesting than you know. Deep within you is a "Kreative." Like the Kraken, it is a superpower that needs to be released. Three steps to releasing the Kreative: 1) Take a step, 2) Keep moving, and 3) Resistance is acceptable.

King Sverre Sigurdsson of Norway in 1180 told his departing sailors to be wary of a large tentacled beast off of the shores. These words constitute the first recorded account of the Kraken.[132]

From that point on, a monstrous tentacled beast has been described in the fictions of Jules Verne, Victor Hugo, Alfred Tennyson, and a great many fathers who came back from a fishing trip. The Kraken is a thing of myth and legend

———

132 "The Real-Life Origins of the Legendary Kraken."
2015. The Conversation.

included in pop culture staples including Pirates of the Caribbean 2, Clash of the Titans, and 20,000 Leagues Under the Sea. Accounts of this creature are varied and horrifying.

Oceans are a bit horrifying.

In many respects, we know more about our own solar system and galaxy than we do the workings of our oceans. Our planet is over 70 percent water. Our human bodies rely fairly heavily on air, heat, light, and a pretty narrow band of acceptable pressure to survive. In that context, the Earth on which we tend to claim dominance is over 70 percent uninhabitable to us.

The oceans are cold, dark, foreign abysses, about which we have so much we don't know. In an article in *LiveScience* by Tia Ghose from 2012, she cites a report suggesting that even after the thousands of animals we know about in the deeps, as many as two-thirds of the species remain undiscovered or documented.[133] We as a scientific people, exploring and asking questions about our galaxy, don't know who we share a planet with.

The Kraken, a story nearly a thousand years old, stands as a significant embodiment of that fear. Our home, our planet, is actually quite foreign, quite unknown, and even quite deadly.

In Clash of the Titans, the Kraken is used as the atomic option of Zeus. His ward that, when released, comes from the deep to envelop cities and dominate. In both the original 1981

---

133 Ghose, Tia. 2012. "Most Ocean Species Remain Undiscovered." Livescience.Com.

version and the vastly inferior 2010 remake, Zeus gives the order, "Release the KRAKEN!" to besiege upon humanity his displeasure, and it does. From between continental plates emerges a beast that the puny humans can't ignore. The gods are angry. The Kraken is here.

And that is the analogy that will frame this section.

YOU ARE AN OCEAN

You are deeper, far less explored, far more dangerous, and potentially more interesting than you know. You are aware of your satellites, your surroundings, and galaxies. You understand your atmosphere and presence, but very few of us know any more about our depths than scientists know about our oceans. Just so much is there.

But for all of the species we know exist and all the rest we don't, we have a single creature buried deep, waiting for our call of release.

We'll call them our "Kreative."

Like the Kraken was for Zeus, your Kreative is an enveloping ability to take on problems bigger than yourself. It grants resources outside the analytical and gives godlike powers of creation and destruction. When you release and harness your Kreative, you are unstoppable. Problems no longer exist. Neither do objections or obstacles. What remains are monstrous perspective and the ability to devour things that stand in your way.

This idea may sound harrowing and intimidating, and it can be. Creatives throughout history have been mocked, outcast, revered, feared, loved, hated, worshiped, reviled, respected, disrespected, followed, or fired. But, with as of yet no exception, if I can name the person for some contribution to history, they owe it to releasing their Kreative.

TO QUOTE THE VASTLY OVERREFERENCED STEVE JOBS AGAIN:

"Here's to the crazy ones, the misfits, the rebels, the troublemakers, the round pegs in the square holes ... the ones who see things differently—they're not fond of rules. ... You can quote them, disagree with them, glorify or vilify them, but the only thing you can't do is ignore them because they change things... they push the human race forward, and while some may see them as the crazy ones, we see genius, because the ones who are crazy enough to think that they can change the world, are the ones who do."[134]

—STEVE JOBS (WORDS BY JOHN "APPLESEED" CHAPMAN)

This quote describes the mentality of many, but the actions of few. Why is that?

Is it really antiquated biological fear holding people back? How do we release the Kreative?

Are we waiting for someone to come along and write a system-based analytical checklist for approaching things in a new way?

---

134 Marshall, Carrie, and MacFormat 265. 2013. "The Appleseed Legend: The Story Behind Apple's Unofficial Mascot." TechRadar.

"In this text, you will see my seven-step system for turning your company from awful to awesome using a formularized system of looking at things in a new way" or some equally flawed approach to fixing a problem with a set solution.

But KIRK! There must be steps—there must be some approach to being one of Steve Jobs' "misfits"!

Back again to perspective. People are so afraid of the ocean's depths they paint all problems with simple, standardized solutions. Systems let them feel control over something they have literally no control over:

These seven steps will help you, and if they don't, the problem must be you.

Books, articles, blogs, libraries of information drawing parameters around a single perspective in an attempt to formularize chaos and standardize what can't be standardized. The notion is quite trendy, and who doesn't love a good trend? I hope you find my three-step attempt illuminating.

Release the Kreative —

Step 1: Take a step. In any direction. The distance between that thing you want and you having it is movement. You have to be moving to get anywhere. The best path between any two points is almost never a straight line, so don't worry too much if after that one step you are actually a bit further from your goal.

If you ask the popular map app Waze for directions, it will take you on some pretty insane routes through what can be really unconventional-seeming roads. While using Waze, I've gone off on dirt trails, cut through parking lots, traveled for miles through suburban neighborhoods off the main roads, and on more than one occasion gone in literally the opposite direction of my destination. But Waze has seldom led me wrong. The path might look insane, it might be unconventional, it might be indirect, and it might seem inconvenient, but it is getting you there.

This concept isn't new, just often forgotten and, for the most part, wildly out of practice. The Persian poet Jalāl ad-Dīn Muhammad Rūmī (most often referred to simply as Rumi) lived in what is now Afghanistan from 1207 to 1273. Like Plato, Socrates, and Aristotle, his wisdom is still largely applicable today, but not as widely circulated in Western culture, for reasons I don't dare attempt to rationalize here.

He said:

"As you start to walk on the way, the way appears."[135]

The statement might seem glib and like a prefabricated Pinterest motivational meme, but remarkably often we find that only once we start actually walking, do we find the path. Only while pushing in ANY direction do we figure out what

---

135   As his original poems were in various languages and a multitude of works, a single source or verified account was not found.

the right direction is. Don't let "analysis paralysis" keep you from doing anything.

In going after your goals, the situation will never be perfect; it will rarely even be ideal. If you wait for the stars to align, you will rarely be ready if they do.

If you take a step and it turns out to be "backward," that's fine—at least you're moving. Momentum counts for a lot more than you realize.

Step 2: Keep moving and adjust as necessary.

Walt Disney once said:

"Around here, however, we don't move backwards for very long. We keep moving forward, opening up new doors and doing new things ... and curiosity keeps leading us down new paths."[136]

The world is full of resources, experts, friends, peers, mentors, teachers, guides, shamans, and gurus. Follow the paths that lead to your goal, and avoid situations that try and define your goal for you.

You have depths of knowledge you aren't using; you have perspectives you have been told are wrong, or misguided, or irrelevant—start with those. Find the path that resonates for you.

---

136 Zipkin, Nina. 2016. "16 Inspirational Quotes From Walt."

Every single thing that gets in your way, celebrate it. Your obstacles are not impediments, but rather steps that shoot you higher as you propel yourself over them.

Moving backward is actually fine, if doing so helps you orient yourself to your goals, your path, your objective. It is actually fine to move laterally or diagonally toward a goal. Just keep moving. Open doors. Figure it out.

Yes, this advice sounds like "rah-rah" motivational speak. But with a Kreative perspective of a problem, putting away the fear you know is completely irrational, every fence you have to climb is just strength training for the next one. Release the Kreative. Don't fear the admonition of people happy to be anonymous.

Step 3: Resistance is acceptable. Star Trek has a race of beings called the Borg. Now, whether or not you are familiar with the idiosyncrasies of the species, their terrifying "war cry" was a dispassionate, "You will be assimilated; resistance is futile."

See, the Borg didn't destroy as much as they absorbed others and forced them to be like them. They removed originality, individuality, singularity, and absorbed everything into a collective. Not on quite so literal a level, but that is what a lot of our educations, training, and corporate expectations do as well.

But here is the thing: You are allowed to have an opinion. You are allowed to disagree. You are allowed to voice ideas. You are allowed to look silly and should endeavor to do so. You don't need to assimilate... resistance is acceptable.

Just as Sir Francis Bacon taught with empirical evidence, don't accept things just because you've been told to. Only when you observe and understand. Only when it becomes your perspective should you really worry about it.

"Truth will sooner come out of error
than from confusion."[137]

—SIR FRANCIS BACON

HOW WOULD THIS APPLY?

You were sitting in your cubicle. Your boss gave you that assignment, and you've just noticed something. The task is based off the wrong assumptions. It inherently suggests the existence of a problem you know isn't real, or an occurrence that isn't happening—as if your boss is using a MapQuest printout from 2002 before the city built the new highway and bulldozed that old shopping mall. All the directions are based off data that isn't true, and even if it was, the directions are taking you the wrong way anyway.

Maybe something like that has happened to you. I've certainly experienced such a situation.

Or perhaps:

A client just walked in the door. They have a problem, they know what the problem is, they know what the solution is— they just need your expertise to help. You sit down and they

---

137 Doss, Henry. 2020. "Innovation: A Tale of Language, Marissa Mayer, Francis Bacon And The Sonnet." Forbes.

explain the situation. They tell you why the situation is a problem and why them hiring your services is the solution. And you agree. The problem arises from the fact that you don't see their problem as the problem. You agree that they need your services, but not the services they are asking for and certainly not aimed at the vertical they intend.

Perhaps something like this scenario is common for you. It is for me.

But maybe:

You're working with an organization that has been around for decades. It has the data, infrastructure, and leadership of a well-oiled machine. The leaders know what they are doing. Every cog in the mechanism is finely machined to work perfectly. But you see a flaw. It isn't egregious or life-threatening. But it certainly is a loss of efficiency or opportunity. Fixing the flaw, albeit innocuous and benign, if nothing else will make certain functions more effective, but this organization doesn't want to be told they are behind. They cornered this market when you were still in school.

Maybe you've seen that. I have.

"I don't know what to do,
But I know what needs to be done."

—ANONYMOUS

If you want something to change, you have to change something.

What do you do? How do you handle it? Do you say something? Do you go to your boss? Do you write up the proposal?

OR do you assume they know something you don't? Do you assume you must be wrong? Do you assume that if you say something you'll just be ridiculed or ignored? How do you thread the needle? How do you make sure you are heard and also that your opinion is relevant to the organization?

Step 1: Take a step. It doesn't have to be dramatic or noteworthy. Write an email, gather data, learn what you can, ask your boss to clarify. Set up an appointment to talk about the issue. Literally no wrong answer exists other than "keep my head down."

Step 2: Keep moving and adjust as necessary. After Step 1, something happened. Maybe a dead end, maybe a new piece of information, maybe a new resource. Follow it down the rabbit hole. Just keep moving.

Step 3: Resistance is acceptable. Your boss might glower at you; your coworkers might look at you weird. You might have to explain what you mean repeatedly. All of these results are okay and serve as indications that people see you in action. Many might offer advice, and some of it might be good. People will resist change. That doesn't mean we shouldn't change.

— Then KEEP GOING—

This is Part 3. Here we talk about people who are taking steps. Not in history, but now. Their contributions might not be particularly insane or noteworthy, but their work is trying to change the way people think. Not in huge, sweeping, billion-dollar ways, but in reasonable, measurable, understandable ways.

They have released their Kreative and are, thus, very fun to watch.

CHAPTER SEVENTEEN

CINNAMON SNAPS, SYNAPSE, AND SYNONYMS

———

TL;DR—Misaligned memories are the cornerstone of creativity. Changing the information that we have, or the context in which we look at things, encourages creative thought.

A song by the band Sister Hazel in the year 2000 received so much airplay that it became one of those songs you heard in your dreams and found yourself humming, almost involuntarily. It featured the hook:

"If you want to be somebody else,
if you're tired of fighting battles with yourself,
if you want to be somebody else
Change Your Mind."

The song is great, and even offers good advice as far as clever turns of phrase go, but as far as actionable advice? It leaves quite a bit wanting.

Again, to wave my pedantic wand... what do you mean by "change your mind"? Are we talking hypnosis? Therapy? Blunt force trauma? If our only source of processing information is our mind, then processing a different way to process becomes a nonsensical loop of circular logic quite quickly. I mean, I guess we could consider brain surgery.

I understand that Ken Block likely never intended his lyrics to be applied quite so literally, but the song sparks an actual question. How would you "change your mind"? I don't mean in the "chicken or fish" debate, or the question that haunts my dreams, "cake or pie?" But more ... how do you change? Can you change? If you want to stop being X or be more Y, can you?

YES? SORT OF? SEEMS TO BE. A DEFINITE MAYBE!

Stepping back from the drastic "behavioral brain surgery" to just "brain science," we can see dozens of specialties unentangling and analyzing the individual fragments of the brain, how they can be tracked, affected, influenced and even ultimately "changed."

Psychology, psychiatry, neuroscience, neuropsychology, neurobiology, cognitive science, cognitive psychiatry—the list really does go on into what seem like infinite subgenres and specialties. The brain may just be the most ineffable thing we know about, and interestingly enough the only thing in existence we know of that named itself.

Change your mind?

Be more creative, be more innovative, think more effectively outside the box—for our purposes, that is the goal. Where do we start? How do you become more creative? Or more innovative?

If creativity, conformity, and innovation are a byproduct of how you process information, and the core physiology of how you process information is somewhat inaccessible, the easiest entry point would seem to be the information, not the process.

"Invention, my dear friends, is 93 percent perspiration, 6 percent electricity, 4 percent evaporation, and 2 percent butterscotch ripple."
—WILLIE WONKA AND THE CHOCOLATE FACTORY (1971)

Start with the information

Unlike "invention," innovation isn't particularly self-explanatory nor easy to define. Even the multiple dictionaries I referenced were malleable and ambiguous regarding a succinct and distinct definition. How do you more definitively define a word for, "I found if I changed the sequence in which I did the task I was more effective and efficient"?

Succinctly summarizing a cognitive accomplishment really is difficult.

"I had a thought, it was good?"

Synonyms are always a little baffling. "Invention" and "innovation" aren't strictly synonyms. "Migrate" and "travel" don't mean the same thing, and neither do contingent and dependent, yet we often treat them as interchangeable.

There is a fairly good chance that, unless you're a foodie, or you aren't from North America, you've never actually had "true" cinnamon—Ceylon cinnamon, because Cassia, a different species with a different country of origin, different temperament, different texture, and most importantly different flavor, is what is sold under the name "cinnamon" in the grocery stores and markets in, at least, the United States.[138] Not the same thing, but we slap the word on it and pretend it is.

Innovation occurs when a person with a unique experience and background strains their knowledge through their perspective, drawing connections from the myriad eclectic, seemingly unassociated data to form new connections, new processes, and new results.

Without getting into how to change the process, a huge step toward innovation is adding more disassociated and

---

138 "Ceylon Vs. Cassia — Not All Cinnamon Is Created Equal."
    2020. Healthline.

inapplicable information. A semester of underwater basket weaving, culinary history, or a master class in calligraphy might serve you quite well as a CPA, a lawyer, or midlevel project manager.

Truly, you might muse on the theory of relativity while working as a patent clerk. Your paradigm-altering breakthroughs might actually be because of your time working on other stuff, not in spite of it. With more information, available data, and general world insights and experiences, your perspective shifts and gives your process more to go on.

If "your process" has the information, the knowledge, it has more options for connections. However, how much you've been taught doesn't matter if you don't remember it. Wisdom comes from understanding and applying, which ties back to memory, right? Knowledge only reaches wisdom of your perspective if it makes into your process and stays there.

Therefore, if memory is tied to wisdom and perspective through knowledge, is it tied to creativity?

Here is an old Russian saying:

"Everything new is just well forgotten old."

Is creativity just remembering old stuff and reapplying it?

Enter Dr. Carmen Simon

Dr. Carmen Simon is a cognitive neuroscientist, a leading expert on memory, a sought-after speaker and the founder of Memzy, a consultancy that helps organizations make compelling, memorable, dynamic content.

It is not an unfair statement to say I am a fan of Dr. Carmen Simon. Her book Impossible to Ignore is recognized as a leading text on the subject of communication through content. It reframed how I thought about thinking; it changed how I looked at memory and creativity. It led me to ask a lot of questions.

There was just one thing to do: call her.

"Are you as creative as the strength of your memories?"

That was her question to me.

"I'm sorry, I'm not sure I understand" was my response.

I had described my thesis to Dr. Simon, "making friends with the mouse," and my proposed ridiculous hypothetical solutions.

What about a mouse fence?
What about a supersonic frequency?
What about a medieval piper that could lure the mice away?
What if we could make friends with the mouse? (I proposed, probably too eagerly.)

She then explained what had truly never occurred to me about innovation:

Each of my proposed solutions, was a memory:

- I've seen a fence. I know what one looks like; I know how they work.
- I've heard of dog whistles and have seen the 1978 Superman, so I'm pretty much an expert on supersonic frequencies.
- I've, of course, heard the story of the Pied Piper luring the RATS (and children) away.
- As the father of five children, I am remarkably aware of Cinderella and her ability to have rodents do her housework. (Just clean your room! No! MICE CAN'T HELP YOU.)

Memories misaligned

My ideas, intentionally ridiculous and meant to be a far-fetched example of thinking outside of the box, didn't "create" nor solve anything. Were they creative? Were they innovative? Were they just ridiculous?

Most appropriately, Dr. Simon explains they are actually "intentionally misaligned memories." I was taking things from one context and applying them to another. Innovations and creativity, it would seem, are just that. The combining understanding from a breadth of experiences, and trying things in new categories, putting round pegs in square holes just to see if they, for some reason, actually fit.

To reference Peter Drucker's quote again:

"We know now that the source of wealth is something specifically human: knowledge.

If we apply knowledge to tasks we already know how to do, we call it 'productivity'.

If we apply knowledge to tasks that are new and different, we call it 'innovation'.

Only knowledge allows us to achieve these two goals."

What Peter Drucker calls "knowledge," Dr. Simon refers to as "memory," as knowledge really is just what we remember of our experiences and educations. Memories and knowledge applied become productivity or innovation.

But if creativity is memories (or knowledge) intentionally misused, shouldn't there be a way to "change your mind" or "hack" your creativity, so to speak?

Yes!

A lot of people extol the merits of "exercising your creative muscle" and "growing your creativity," and that idea is absolutely right. Just the simple act of thinking "creatively" can lead to more creative thought. In their own way, those individuals are recommending we practice "misaligning our memories."

But that isn't what I mean:

Story Time:

When I was a young child, I loved the work of a particular novelist [for various privacy concerns, I won't include his name or those of his works in this book]. I poured over his stories like children a decade later would cling to Harry Potter. In many ways, my developmental understanding of storytelling was learned within his fiction.

When I matured to the ripe and wizened age of "high school junior," I was having an existential crisis about college majors and what direction I was going to take in life. I remember things the author had said in interviews about how he became the storyteller he was. I wanted to be a storyteller—filmmaker—and he was the best storyteller ever, so HE was going to have the answer.

It was the late '90s, the internet wasn't a big thing yet, but 411 was in full swing, and not many people knew how to block their number. I realize this story makes me sound crazy, but I called him.

I told him I wanted to be a filmmaker, but that I heard majoring in film was a "dead end" and I wasn't sure how to proceed.

He told me,

"If you want to be filmmaker, study ANYTHING but filmmaking. If you want to tell a story, you need a story to tell."

He told me I needed to collect life experiences, knowledge, a breadth of understanding, and that is how I would become the best storyteller ever. Armed with the wisdom of the creator of my childhood heroes and a newfound passion for storytelling, I promptly enrolled in film school. Yeah, I know … I know.

My major ended up being in business with a concentration in entertainment, and remarkably film focused. I knew films backward and forward, I understood the technical, theoretical, and philosophical aspects, but as I'd been warned … I had little more to say.

Knowledge = memories, and misaligned memories = creativity = innovation.

I'd spent the entirety of my education (and most of my life for that matter) storing up facts about filmmaking. I developed memories and systems for business and the entertainment industry. I hyper focused my life toward the understanding of Hollywood and what made it tick. I built up my experiences, memories, insights, and practices within a very narrow field.

This expertise made me a relatively proficient specialist, but it deprived me of a creative frame of reference. I was the "go-to guy" for a remarkably specific set of things, within a remarkably specific set of parameters. But I hadn't primed myself with potential innovation. I wasn't bringing anything new to the conversation.

I didn't have any diversity to my knowledge, or any outside applications or insights from a different perspective. All I knew I'd learned from people within the industry. All I did had been graded and approved by people who had done this work before. That should sound like a good thing, and it is in some ways. However, it limited my frame of reference to the world as others had seen it.

If you watch many movies, specifically if you watch many lower budget/student films, this problem is actually fairly common. It's why so many independent films are about someone making an independent film. These are creatively inclined people, pulling from a narrow focus. These individuals are inherently creative, but like I had inadvertently done, have deprived themselves the breadth you need for real creativity. They didn't have memories to misalign, or at least ... I didn't.

Reframing History

If we apply the real genius and contribution of Aristotle, Plato, and Socrates, we see they were students of everything, with diverse understanding and diverse studies, applying observations and assumptions across schools of thoughts to develop new ways of approaching an issue.

"Misaligned Memories" can be used to describe both Henry Ford and Frank Stephenson, as well as others. Creativity, innovation, big breakthroughs all come, in some part, from "misaligned memories" or, more simply put, unrelated knowledge.

Inventions like the device that made mustard more efficient may come from deep-rooted specialty in a specific field. But to break the paradigm, you have to have a frame of reference from outside of it.

Real innovations and new ways of thinking in many ways are just reorganizations, expansions, and realignments of a breadth of knowledge. Sir Francis Bacon, Sir Isaac Newton, and the Royal Society questioned and studied everything. Their goal: to understand all of the known universe. They take into account not just hyperspecialized sciences, but a breadth of understanding in all things.

They innovated by crossing understandings, restructuring knowledge, and questioning everything they knew, then applying everything they found out to everything else they found out.

Maybe not in the way that we tend to think of "creatives," but by the sheer process of applying knowledge outside of its core function across other disciplines. This approach is creative thought. Memories (data), misaligned.

LIBERAL ARTS? CROSS-DISCIPLINARY EDUCATION?

"Misaligned memories" could be described as another way of saying "cross-disciplinary" or a "liberal arts education," and it both is and isn't. "Cross-disciplinary" usually implies someone with an MBA/JD or PhD/MD or even JD/MBA. It refers to someone with multiple specialties, a breadth spanning more than one area of expertise. That is certainly included here. However, those areas are still applied fields of study, taught by professors and industries with standards and practices.

To make true creativity, innovation, and disruption possible with misaligned memories, you'd need to be more like a lawyer who is also a beekeeper, or jazz musician, or backyard wrestler.

This idea was the original concept of "liberal arts education" that is essentially dead in all but name in modern era. Liz Coleman, president of Bennington College, has spoken at length about this, including in her 2009 TED Talk.

"We have professionalized liberal arts to the point where they no longer provide the breadth of application and the enhanced capacity for civic engagement that is their signature. Over the last century, the 'expert' has dethroned the educated generalist to become the sole model of intellectual accomplishment."[139]

—LIZ COLEMAN

We talk in business of silos, the fractioning of information, and the responsibility and problems it causes. But our society is encouraging, and even requiring, siloing ourselves. Vast expertise required in small areas, and "wasted" education ridiculed for its "inapplicability."

What Aristotle, Sir Frances Bacon, and Henry Ford did to gather a breadth of understanding is being put into smaller and smaller "expert" boxes, leading us to need more and more expert building blocks to round out a think tank to fill even a single set of ideas.

---

139 Coleman, Liz. 2020. "A Call to Reinvent Liberal Arts Education." Ted.Com.

THINK OUTSIDE THE BOX? IS THERE A BOX?

We could reasonably say from Dr. Simon's methodologies that two basic steps to "hacking" your creativity exist, outside of just "practice being creative."

1. Collect experiences and knowledge. Take pictures, do things, learn as much as you can about as much as you can. Keep a journal. Go as broad or as deep as you dare. Learn new things; collect unique perspectives and differences of opinion. Study failure. See what didn't work.

2. Go back and reflect on those things. Keep your memory active. Keep the diversity of your mental resources alive.

You can only make friends with the mouse if you have a frame of reference for it. You can only "think outside the box" if you've found the edges, scaled them, and peered down the other side.

CHAPTER EIGHTEEN

YOU ARE WHO YOUR FRIENDS ARE

TL;DR—"The persona model" used in communication was a brilliant and helpful tool that has largely seen its day. Dr. Denise Gosnell uses graph data to find a new way of understanding gathered information. We need to be willing to throw out "industry standards" that can be improved upon.

A great many things stay in practice long past their relevance. Entire industries hold to standards, some not knowing why, only that it is the standard. Practices are put in place for solid reasons, but the reasons move on and the practice remains.

We can see examples of this phenomenon in almost every industry and institution, just as our friend Sir Francis Bacon moved against the top universities in the world, the elite, teaching the successful albeit antiquated methods of the past.

Whether standards and practices remain or are reintroduced and rehashed for historic reasons, political reasons, or personal reasons of the leadership, practices that don't hold to modern efficacy need to be sought out and addressed.

While studying communications at Georgetown University, I was repeatedly reintroduced to a particular practice: "personas." I questioned them every time to every professor who brought them up. I asked how it made sense to continue to work with this model when everything we had rendered it not only semi-useless, but on my more aggressive days, embarrassingly antiquated.

I had no shortage of professors and industry professionals continue to explain their merit. As I would question it, often repeatedly, they would continue to say, "just watch—it'll all make sense."

What did eventually make sense was this: every one of them would eventually say, "this is just the way it works."

For what it's worth, there is some truth to that, but butter churns work too, and that fact doesn't make them the best tool for the job.

"There's three ways to do things: the right way, the wrong way, and the way that I do it."

—ROBERT DE NIRO, CASINO, 1995

Personas: My Villain

For those who don't work in the field of communications, or some user-side software development, allow me to give you the ten-cent tour of personas. In this practice, a communicator, PR professional, marketer, etc. would develop a model of an ideal customer, based on basic targeting and assumed demographic data. First introduced by Alan Cooper in his 1999 book, The Inmates are Running the Asylum,[140] the purpose was to set boundaries and give shape to a proposed user of various software. Limiting a software design to the confines of a "real person" helped get away from "elastic users" as he called them, or users who could change or shift on a whim.

While researching them to better understand where they came from, I came upon a statement by Alan Cooper himself that helped me much better conceptualize where the idea began.

"The book was intended to alert managers to the problems inherent in designing software for use by non-engineers. It was never meant as a 'how-to' book for interaction designers. However, at the time the practice of interaction design was relatively unknown, and my methods in particular were so unfamiliar, I felt it necessary to add some description of the Goal-Directed methodology. My goal was simply to demonstrate that there was indeed some substance to my method: that it was different, that it was effective, that it was real."[141]

---

140 Alan Cooper, "The Inmates are Running the Asylum," 1999 Sams
141 "The Origin Of Personas." 2008. Cooper.

And it did work for early "interaction designers" such as marketers, who had previously also had a problem unifying messaging for teams.

In the Mad Men era of marketing (generally speaking the '50s to '90s, between the household integration of the television and the internet), companies got essentially no feedback. You placed ads on the radio, in a newspaper, or on television and watched revenue. No tool in practice could tie the two sets of data to each other. No one had a reliable way to gauge if marketing efforts were having any significant impact.

The new "persona" model was a revolutionary way to visualize a specific person. It was misaligned, primed to be used for an unintended purpose, and quickly adapted to be a standard industry practice of marketing and advertising.[1]

While it didn't provide any feedback, it gave edges and form to a practice, which up to that point was just broadcasting out a message into the void, hoping to see results rise from the ether.

This model was a genuine innovation to the approach, practices, thinking, and methods for twenty years of communication.

EXAMPLE:

Previously: Marketing something for the home, you could choose to market that product to "working moms," and that was it. Add some general data based on the type of product—for example, based on price it is going to be used in these social segments more than others, etc.

Persona model: Meet Diane, a thirty-nine-year-old mother of three. Her oldest is twelve, and her youngest is starting kindergarten next year. She works as an attorney practicing corporate real-estate law. The family has a dog and two cats. Diane has been married for fifteen years; her husband is an executive of a small financial management firm.

She has a hard time managing the multiple schedules and responsibilities of being a mother and working professional. She has an executive assistant at work and remarkable child care, but the many requirements of being a mom, executive, and wife really wear her down.

It cost nothing. It wasn't technology. It didn't require special training. It was simply a new way of framing the conversation. A way of visualizing the problem differently. With it, many companies and teams found remarkable success in unifying their message. It proved an invaluable tool for many, but it was firmly rooted in a mentality of "above the line media" from the previous generation.

Given my adoration for misaligned ideas and alternative methodologies and tech, my distaste for personas is admittedly a tad hypocritical.

But I'm not alone in my criticism, which is that while this model solved the problem of an "elastic user," it created the problem of marketing a product to a potentially stereotyped effigy that may or may not be indicative of the actual audience or customer for a desired message.

Simply put, this person is your imaginary friend, this is who you want your audience to be, even who you plan your audience to be. This model helped marketers and communicators visualize the audience. It made the audience feel "real" and become sometimes very beloved—however, as irony would have it, the practice that made the audience feel "real" lacked emotional nuance that makes a person interesting. Any and all nuance applied was fictitious.

Personas weren't real and weren't necessarily who your audience actually was.[142]

Why use a shotgun when we have laser beams?

The humorous, almost tragic part of personas is the timing. Their incorporation into the communication process, for which they weren't intended, as a way of resonating with masses without feedback, was right, as new technology was providing the audience feedback that marketing communicators had never had.

We would very soon know information about our consumer we never had access to in the past. In the very near future

---

142 "Personas – A Simple Introduction." 2020. The Interaction Design Foundation.

(of 1999), we would be able to know anything and everything we wanted to.

But armed with this new methodology borrowed from software designers, marketers and communicators doubled down into the world of their perceived customer rather than using their actual one.

These two brand-new trains of thought (internet feedback and persona development) grew in tandem, tenuous bridges of data being utilized by analysts and data scientists connecting and/or empowering personas with data to support assumptions. But personas were largely built on historic demographic research and Jungian archetypes (a methodology of categorizing people devised by Carl Jung in the late 1800s).

Meanwhile, over the last twenty years, data has become our friend. We now know more than ever before; we can see not just who our customer is, but where they are, when they are, why they are, and, as turned out to be the most important feature, who their friends are.

Dr. Denise Gosnell, PhD, a data scientist with a concentration in algorithms and graph-structured data, tracks and utilizes data to prove and demonstrate people's identity on social networks. She works daily with the persona model, but specifically in proving who users really are, and in essence tracking and predicting behavior using the same dataset we've had access to for the majority of the life of the persona model, just applying new ways of thinking around it. No new tech, just new ways of interpreting data we've often been ignoring for more than two decades.

Churn and Burn

Persona models and data models are used to visualize, categorize, and attempt to solve all of big businesses' many issues. One such problem for nearly all industries is customer churn, when a customer of any length of time leaves your service for that of your competitor. In some industries, the lifetime value and loyalty of customers is more valuable than in others.

In larger, long-term-contract-type business models, customer churn proves a real problem. Many Fortune 500 companies have spent significant amounts of money researching and combatting the problem of customer churn, needing to understand what they can do to maintain loyalty, to establish longer-term customer relationships.

Modern telecommunications companies (i.e., the catch-all of your identity you carry in your pocket, your cell phone) are a prime example. Phone carriers have been in what has seemed like an all-out consumer war since the landline era, when commercials for AT&T, Sprint, and MCI barraged the airwaves while the same companies battled in court over antitrust, innovations, and government-supported monopolies (but I digress).

Data-driven decisions

In the past, within the older paradigm of data research and the persona model, when companies analyzed customer churn, the questions that would be asked would be first basic demographics:

- Age,
- Income,
- Gender,
- Geographic location,
- Etc.

After that, they would dig deeper into behaviors:

- Did they pay their bill last month?
- The month before?
- What did their cell phone usage look like?
- How often were they making calls?
- To how many unique numbers?

A quality metric could be ascribed on X and Y axes: X being number of uses of a cell phone in one week, Y number of unique encounters. This data is of particular significance as it, unlike other behavioral data, has been available for significantly longer than the twenty years of residential access to the internet.

Graphing this data would show behavior mixed with demographic data to afford you a "solid" understanding of the real customer. You can now see who this person is. But it turns out, with other data we already had, we can apply a whole different line of logic that shows a much more leading edge of information as far as prediction of customer churn:

"You are who your friends are."

—DR. DENISE GOSNELL, PHD

Not just how many calls and to how many unique numbers, but more:

- How many repeat numbers?
- What networks are you calling most often?
- Are the people you are talking to on the same type of device as you?
- Are they on the same network?
- Are they in the same city?
- Are their behaviors similar to yours?

By building a model that graphs a social group as opposed to an individual, we are able to far better predict behavior. You are who your friends are.

Graphing groups as individuals identifies the key outliers in the group. Statistically, that outlier is the person who is about to churn, from wherever they are, to wherever their group is.

"And by just taking the exact same data, but looking at it differently, these companies were able to increase their churn model ... for certain types of people moving up to being 98% accurate and ... able to predict when a customer would churn."

—DR. DENISE GOSNELL, PHD

In the case of telecommunications companies, this approach wasn't new data, only a new way of looking at it and an interest in new associations and graphs that were always there but overlooked. As Dr. Gosnell points out, the data is there and shows far more than we've ever noticed.

Old information, old methodology, reworked into a new approach

In the Mad Men era, we aimed our ads at the ether and without feedback watched revenue, hoping the two were related. Under the innovation of personas, we added a shape and personality to the audience. This tactic gave communicators a better feel for the message and let them feel they were more connected to their audience.

It offered little in the way of feedback, but this change of thought allowed for great success (or at least perceived success) toward landing and affecting an audience.

But by rethinking the problem, adding data that we have access to, and asking better questions, we can draw conclusions never seen before.

"Modeling it that way, to see what other types of trends that they're finding data driven innovation, by just looking at a different dimension that's already in your data—I guess all the tools we've been using up until now did not let you see that type of layer."

—DR. DENISE GOSNELL, PHD

It adds the nuance to the personas that the Jungian archetypes and demographics lacked. By changing our mind, we have a new horizon in communications.

Maybe I'm wrong

I do not understand the obsession with and adherence to the persona model. I don't fathom why you'd overlook data about your customer to talk to an effigy you hope is listening.

But maybe I'm wrong. Looking at a problem differently doesn't make your way sacrosanct, just different. I don't understand the persona model, but thousands of people find it remarkably helpful. It is a tool, and valuable for some.

But just as Bill Gates explained to his quorum of European bankers: let's move to tomorrow where we have access to new frontiers of data and put away our toys.

The persona model is a proven methodology. But I promise: it will die. Personas have had a useful tenure as our imaginary friend, but in years to come, we'll be onto something else. We'll find other methods, other ideas. New data. New people and approaches. Don't get attached to the tool of yesterday.

Today is already tomorrow.

CHAPTER NINETEEN

REALITY TV IS STRANGER THAN FICTION

TL;DR—TV is a great tool for communicating society, badly. Ideas translated quickly across the world divide attention, reduce credibility, and create problems. Creative businesses have a harder time with creatives, not an easier one. To overcome a creative roadblock, become a point of gravity.

If I might brazenly steal from one of my favorite writers of television or any other medium, Aaron Sorkin, from his 1999 show Sports Night:

William H. Macy as Sam Donovan: "You guys know who Philo Farnsworth was? … He invented television. I don't mean he invented television like Uncle Milty. I mean he invented the television, in a little house in Provo, Utah, at a time when the idea of transmitting moving pictures through the air would be like me saying I figured out a way to beam us aboard the Starship Enterprise.

"He was a visionary. He died broke and without fanfare. The guy I really like, though, was his brother-in-law, Cliff Gardner.

"He said, 'Philo, I know everyone thinks you're crazy, but I want to be a part of this. I don't have your head for science, so I'm not going to be able to help much with the design and mechanics of the invention, but it sounds like you're going to need glass tubes.'

"You see, Philo was inventing the cathode receptor, and even though Cliff didn't know what that meant or how it worked, he'd seen Philo's drawing, and he knew that he was gonna need glass tubes. And since television hadn't been invented yet, it's not like you could get them at the local TV repair shop.

"'I want to be a part of this,' Cliff said. 'I don't have your head for science. How would it be if I were to teach myself to be a glass blower? And I could set up a little shop in the backyard. And I could make all the tubes you'll need for testing.'

"There ought to be congressional medals for people like that."
—SEASON 2 EPISODE 3, "LOUISE REVISITED,"
ORIGINAL AIRDATE 10/19/1999

From its inception and creation by Philo Farnsworth in the early twentieth century, the television has had a very interesting history and application in modern culture. Whether you subscribe to "art imitates life" or "life imitates art," people tend to use the media produced by an era to imagine the prevailing lifestyle of that era.

TV can be a solid measuring stick. It certainly helps us gauge the fashion, general speech, and some of the overall sensibilities of a particular segment of society.

But once you start factoring in the history of censorship, racism, sexism, etc., media can often actually be a more bizarro representation of an era/people/timeframe than a documentation of it. At best, it is an idealization or defamation of the period. At worst, it is the approved histories sanctioned by the thought police.

To add insult to potential injury, not all media is the same, intended to be the same, used the same, aimed the same, or regarded the same. From behind the cameras, the differences in motivations can be pretty clear. However, to the consumer at home ... it all comes across almost exactly the same: moving pictures from a lighted box.

It's easy to dismiss this notion and say, "No, to a mature adult, the differences between entertainment media and news media are clear." However, from a cognitive standpoint and the way the brain absorbs information, this idea isn't always the case at any age, education level, experience level, or even perspective.

"I had a TV show called The Apprentice and it's one of the most successful reality shows in the history of television. And now I'm doing something else."[143]

—PRESIDENT DONALD TRUMP

45TH PRESIDENT OF THE UNITED STATES

Growing up, I remember thinking you could always tell the difference on TV of what was "real" and what was "fiction." The barometer was really simple: boring old people droning on about other boring old people = real. Everything else = fiction. I liked the fiction bits better.

But my perspective as a child was very obviously flawed. The reality was both far simpler and simultaneously far more complicated than that. The real truth was all of it was a bit of both.

The news contained a lot of opinions and sometimes mistakes, and the fiction bits had a lot of strong academic, historical, moral, and ethical constructs. However, the answer being that it's always both and never very clear makes it all a lot harder to parse out.

This leads to a real problem in the world of

Good ideas versus bad ideas.

A famed episode of Crossfire featured comedian and Daily Show host Jon Stewart in an all-out debate with host Tucker Carlson.[144]

---

143 "Interview With Donald Trump." 2016. The Daily News.
144 "Jon Stewart On Crossfire." 2020. YouTube.

The clip has circulated the internet and globe a few hundred times, so if you haven't seen it, please Google it and decide whose side you most align with.

Jon Stewart's point in a nutshell: Crossfire is hurting America by presenting fallacies as facts and diluting the argument and dialog of the American people with pageantry, spin, and other excess.

Tucker Carlson's point in a nutshell: his show opens balanced debate and extends the conversation, and in that The Daily Show masquerades as a news program, Jon Stewart and his show had a certain responsibility to get facts right and inform responsibly, even if comedically.

Stewart's reply: Mine is a comedy show, no responsibility had at all.

Carlson's reply: You're a dick. (sorry mom, he really did say that)

The segment really does warrant watching if you haven't seen it.

Regardless of which of the two talk show gladiators you get behind, their point is somewhat valid: with all the information we are getting, parsing out reality from fiction is increasingly harder.

This issue led us to the era in which we currently live, where we could very easily, albeit cynically, argue that the differences between your favorite talking head pundit from either side of the aisle and reality TV show sensation *Duck Dynasty* are both equally fact and fiction.

This assertion brings together many if not most of the ideas we've talked about up to this point.

Television, the internet, and modern media are bringing together new ways of thinking, new processes, new outlooks, new lifestyles, new options and new behaviors of ever-diversifying groups. They present and represent so many opinions and people with such loud voices that watching or reading requires a shrewd and critical eye.

This phenomenon causes us to eliminate and disregard credible sources, and often to elevate someone's intelligence for reasons wholly unrelated but emotionally held. It causes us, in many ways, to give credit for things where credit doesn't belong and place blame where it doesn't belong either.

It creates cathartic realities where we live vicariously through our own selected heroes and eliminate other equally or more credible sources. But more than most, in my experience, the glitz, the glamour, the louder voices serve to make many people feel less informed, less intelligent, less capable, and less creative.

That isn't "creativity"

Creativity, innovation, and misaligned memories don't give us free reign on the truth. To once again reference the quote by the late Sen. Daniel Patrick Moynihan:

"I'm fine with you having your own opinions, but you can't have your own facts."

The modern internet bringing us an infinite number of channels and giving everyone a global stage has led to an even further blurring of reality and fiction.

We could reasonably say that today's reality TV is as honest a depiction of modern life as Leave It to Beaver or I Love Lucy was an accurate representation of those eras. The difference, I believe, is the scale of it.

Media moguls from Joseph Pulitzer and William Randolph Hearst to, in the more modern world, Ted Turner and Rupert Murdoch got to play with the lines. Now, anyone with Instagram can.

HOW DOES A KREATIVE GET CREATIVE?

My first career was in the film and television industry. That is where I grew to love the "best idea wins" mentality held by many. But in the last decade or so, less creativity seems to come from Hollywood and more explosion-ridden retellings of Grimm's fairytales and comic books on the big screen, and reality TV competition shows and manufactured drama on the little screen.

Troy DeVolld literally wrote the book on reality TV.

No, really, he did: the bestselling definitive guide is called *Reality TV: An Insider's Guide to TV's Hottest Market* by Troy DeVolld. I reached out to him to talk about unleashing creativity in an industry that is already heralded for its creativity.

Troy's career doesn't read terribly differently than many other young, ambitious, wide-eyed creatives set to take the world by storm. The prevailing difference was timing. As Troy entered the world on truly the lowest rung possible, a person who watches hours of reality TV footage and logs if anything interesting happens, the year was 2000, Survivor was truly taking off, and we were on the very early edge of the soon-to-be reality explosion.

From tape logger to producer in a disproportionately short time, Troy transitioned to work on the reality sensation The Osbornes and has been rolling steady ever since. In 2010, he was inducted into his alma mater's, Full Sail University, Hall of Fame.

The grass is always greener on the other side, so how is it the creative center is seeming so "uncreative"?

"TV is now content and product, less than it is innovation, until an innovator comes along and just somehow creates that GRAVITY FIELD around themselves that allows really unusual stuff to get made."

—TROY DEVOLLD

THE DIVIDING LINE THAT ISN'T THERE

Throughout multiple interviews, the reading of numerous books, and an almost obsessive dive into creativity in the workplace, I came upon an assumption, expectation, and observation:

Creativity is important in OTHER fields and offices, not mine.

I work as an xyz, we can't be "creative."

Hollywood, Nashville, NYC—that's where "creatives" are. The rest of us need to do our jobs.

However, a government building full of vested 401(k)s and studio executives answering to investors are essentially the same thing. Quality of the idea, from a content perspective, doesn't really matter.

Whether you are approving the PowerPoint deck for the secretary of commerce, or the rundowns of next season's pilots to the studio head, the name of the game is "don't make them uncomfortable; don't give them a reason to doubt the bottom line."

Loss aversion is real. The chance of making a boatload with a cool new idea for most doesn't outweigh the fear of losing money, prestige, and reputation over a loss. That's our real barrier.

But if we can get past Fear, if we can get past the excuse, the objection … we can be unstoppable.

Fear can't hurt you, and neither can bees.

How do we contend with that?

Our fear of speaking is that we worry about losing the tribe. Our blaming it on not having enough money isn't about having enough money … it's about using any of it on something you're worried might not work. We're afraid of our own credibility being called into question.

But as Troy points out, every so often we have someone enter the stratosphere with innovation. They prove something new. They add facts and a valid case study to the stack of facts and case studies, and if they are lucky they do it in a successful enough way that they create a "gravity field" prompting and promoting others to rush and follow suit.

The situation wasn't that people hadn't before seen "reality TV," which can be tracked to the early days of television and by definition includes Lawrence Welk and Ed Sullivan. In the '90s we had MTV's Road Rules and Real World, and Fox debuted Survivor, all showing us we could fall in love with real people being real. We could make shows without big names, without expensive sets. We could spend much less and make as much or more.

Maybe this concept was about economics, maybe lateral thinking of withered technology. But it absolutely is using misaligned memories, old tech, old styles, old ideas in new ways. Reality TV didn't invent anything, but it changed how content producers approached entertainment.

This sense of awkward reality extended to the big screen as well. Films like *Napoleon Dynamite* (2003) for some were awkward and uncomfortable, and didn't feel like a movie. Jon Heder's representation of what turned out to be a cornucopia of experiences from filmmaker Jared Hess' life resonated with people in a new way. It didn't feel like a movie we'd seen. It was different, simple, without the standard glitz and glamour.

And it spun out its own barrage of similarly toned follow-ups:

Star-studded *Little Miss Sunshine* in 2006.

The unsung film Foot Fist Way, which brought Danny McBride to the world the same year.

Son of Rambow, a great film about an awkward young British friendship making a sequel to their favorite film in 2007.

Scottish ultra-low-budget film Once, which won an Academy Award and was turned into a Broadway and West End musical.

Being awkward and low-budget became really popular—arguably because an odd Idaho childhood and some bootstrap ingenuity made a hit at Sundance in 2003.

Be a point of gravity

It's easy and flippant to attest, "Just be creative and don't care what people say." But fear, even when imagined, is real. *I don't care how harmless they are; I don't like bees.* And we can go in and call our manager or financier or whoever the pocketbook protector may be, and we can passionately demand they pony up the pennies ... but that doesn't always, or even often, work.

But we can see innovators in all fields, be it film/TV or medicine, who are able to make that field of gravity around themselves and change the way the world works.

They change the conversation.

How do they do that?

Emmy Award-winning television writer Brandon Sawyer has worked almost exclusively in animation, writing episodes of The Boss Baby: Back in Business, the movie and television version of The Penguins of Madagascar, Monsters vs. Aliens, and Voltron Force. For a writer, the almost exclusive work product is, at its essence, ideas.

Unlike many of the other talents and trades in the entertainment industry, writing is almost entirely about ideas: who has the best idea, who can make it work "the best."

Brandon and I talked about the world of creative collaboration, "best idea wins" mentality, and the world of creative business:

"You can say best idea wins, but when you're talking about what's funny or even what's moving, or even what's best for story ... it's not an objective thing, where you can say '...this is clearly the best idea.' It's always going to be somebody's opinion

of 'This is the best idea for this moment, or for the story or for the theme.' And you just hope you're working with somebody who shares your taste, and that there's an audience out there that also shares your taste."

That said, establishing yourself as "the point of gravity," and "creative genius" in a room full of would-be "creative geniuses" in this regard seems a much heavier lift.

People in board rooms fear that creativity won't be welcomed, that it is only acceptable in places within creative realms. However, in place of creativity, people are coming from a place of subjective and opinions. You will sometimes have multiple people with multiple good and bad ideas, each with a piece of themselves tied into it.

"People get protective, very understandably ... the passive aggressive emails would go back and forth ... me included, 'but if you did it that way you're going to run into this problem, and you know we should really do it my way.' ...

"But you're always going to lose a lot of battles. It is genuinely hard for me to watch the Penguins movie—and I enjoy that movie, I'm very proud of the work that I did on the movie—but when I watch it, all I see are battles that I lost." [He laughs.] "At this moment or scene ... I still think it would have been better my way." [More laughing.] "But nobody else would experience that. You have to work on something in life enough and lose enough of those battles."

Brandon has failed a lot. He has fought a lot of battles. He has won far more than most who move to Hollywood with dreams of being a star!

Is he a point of gravity? Is he changing the way Hollywood or animation works? Maybe, maybe not.

Troy DeVolld, is he a point of gravity? He's produced twenty-four reality shows and shows no sign of slowing down. Is that permanently affecting the world of reality TV? Possibly, probably not.

But whether Troy or Brandon are changing the world of entertainment is not actually the point. It's to fight for that thing you love. Lose the battles, raise your voice, release the Kreative. Just like we don't know who originally made the Sphinx, making your mark on the world doesn't need to be about credit.

Just about action.

CHAPTER TWENTY

DEFINING GRAVITY: COMMUNICATION AT PLAY

———

TL;DR—Art is communication at play. What happens when your play is communications? Four different case studies of people with artful communications, gravitational pull, and a Kreative mindset.

The Definition of Art

"I have figured it out," he said. "I've been working on this for a few years, and I have had this conversation with a lot of people, and no one has been able to poke any significant hole in it yet."

"The definition of art?" I questioned.

"The OBJECTIVE definition of art," he clarified.

He went on, "Every definition of art, in every dictionary, or given to me by anyone I've asked, is subjective, based on intent or taste. It is amorphous and without form. It can't be codified, defined, or handled in any way."

"Yes, art … is … all those things … sort of," I replied.

Full disclosure: it was after midnight, and this was one of those conversations that can really only be had as a part of a marathon all-night deep dive.

"No, I have figured it out," he repeated. "An objective definition of 'art.'"

"Okay … you have my attention."

"If you think about what 'art' looks like, in all its many forms, or would be described by some outside alien race—how would an anthropologist of another world describe what they saw us doing, as we participated in all the many variations and forms of 'art'?"

"Barely contained hysteria?" (Truth be told, I only thought that, I didn't want to interrupt the flow … but it was my answer.)

"Communication. At. Play." He paused for emphasis. "'Play' has been observed in many species … deer play tag …"

At this point, I'll admit, he was still talking, but my mind was racing. This wasn't "new" information, just a new perspective. I love new perspectives. I sat and thought.

Yes, deer play tag.
Dolphins mess with surfers.
Tigers, lions, wolves, bears play, wrestle, spar, and pounce.
Parrots mock and dance.
Crows and ravens are mischievous pranksters.

"*Play is the fundamental and natural mechanism for learning*," I heard Paul say, somewhat narrating the thoughts as they developed.

Play is a base activity of sentience. Practicing, exploring, growing, developing, expanding, testing, rinse-lather-repeat.

Animals that are predatory "play," stalk, and pounce on their parents and pack mates.

Animals that are social sniff, wrestle, yowl, and nip.

But as we said from the very beginning of this book, people are unique in the animal kingdom: our community, our interactions, our communications.

We communicate. What is art? Us PLAYING with ways to do that. Using different forms to attempt to evoke response and instill emotions.

Dance is a way to express and communicate through movement.
Music communicates through harmonies, melodies, and percussion.

Paintings express feeling, observation, dreams, through pigments and shapes.

The list goes on … and it all tracks.

It might not be a perfect definition, it might need better refining, but I couldn't refute its accuracy. Every form of art I could think of, everything I'd ever done that I considered "art," was me "playing" with a boundary of communication. I was attempting to use my perspective, wit, ideas, or style to express something new.

It was me playing… with communication, media, thinking. That was art.

At this point, I realized he was still talking and while that internal monologue had probably only been eight to ten seconds in real-life time, I felt bad I wasn't listening.

So who was this Arm Chair Philosopher redefining my perspective with his GOOD theory until 3 a.m.?

Mr. Paul Good (yes, really).

MUSIC AND GAMING FESTIVAL

Paul Good heard about the inaugural "Mid-Atlantic Gaming Festival" in 2002. It was new, small, and to his interest. As a man who was a visual effects artist, game designer, and entrepreneur, a fledgling convention speaking to some of his passions did interest him, but … he just didn't have the time.

As weeks went by and he heard of how the first-time festival went, he vowed he wouldn't miss another ... and he hasn't.

In fact, we couldn't really argue that Mr. Good isn't deeply connected and largely responsible for the meteoric rise of the Music and Gaming Festival, or MagFest as it would come to be called.

Festivals and conventions, especially in their early years, are always a bit like herding cats. They have so many more moving pieces than people realize, assume, know, or care to hear about. Con-goers are quick to complain about crowds, lines, and other inconveniences, but the sheer magnitude of even the smallest convention is a pretty significant lift.

Where many people whine and comment from the sidelines, Paul got there year two, saw help was needed, and offered a hand where he could. Year three, he helped out a bit more substantively, and after that he was all-in.

A book could be (and should be) written about the history of Mag-Fest and its incredible journey. I've learned a tremendous amount about its trek and discussed it with the dozens of staff members, volunteers, attendees, and board members I interviewed. But to sum up the brilliance of this organization, I will narrow it down to this:

It seemed (with very few exceptions) that everyone I talked to was a game developer, or someone deep in the IT field. These weren't "party planners," "event organizers," "logisticians," or anything that gave them any "business" running/organizing/hosting/managing a convention.

"We did everything wrong," Paul told me. "On purpose, and we liked it that way. MagFest worked because it was built by computer programmers and set up like a computer game."

I instantly saw what he meant.

I have worked in and around film festivals and comic conventions my whole life, and MagFest absolutely resonates on an entirely different frequency.

Once he pointed this fact out, I could see it. It was set up analytically. Different departments, different interfaces, each going through a motherboard that doled out processing speed, bandwidth, and support as necessary.

While that could be an analogy to describe any festival or convention, the fact that they did it within that mind frame was clear, apparent, and distinctly different.

MagFest deliberately, definitely, and defiantly "reinvented the wheel" of conventions, and the result was something to behold.

MagFest is not without its problems. It is absolutely not devoid of ongoing bugs and viruses (sticking with the analogy), and it still clearly has lines of code that need reworking.

However, 2020 was the eighteenth MagFest. Unlike a vast majority of conventions in this space, it is a nonprofit, run entirely by volunteers: 1,400 passionate and dedicated volunteer staff members, and only eight full-time administrative "employees" to orchestrate Super MagFest, an annual convention of over 20,000 people in the National Capital Area; MagWest, its sister con in San Jose, now in its third year; and MagLabs, which fosters innovation, creation, and general awesomeness. Not to mention current initiatives to expand to Europe and South America.

I haven't done an expansive search, but I know I have never personally encountered an organization that can match that success and track record with an unsubsidized, unsponsored, almost entirely volunteer force.

Ask them how they did it, and people who have been around will happily say: by doing it all wrong, and not caring about the people who told us "the right way to do it."

RELEASE THE KREATIVE FRAMEWORK:
Maybe they didn't know, but they followed very simply my completely unoriginal and in no way proprietary system.

The early founders of MagFest wanted a festival, so they started one:

STEP 1: TAKE A STEP!
The festival didn't go well right away. They didn't know what they were doing. But they figured it out. Not by hiring experts, not by looking up "the right way." They just kept walking the way that made sense for them.

STEP 2: KEEP MOVING AND ADJUST AS NECESSARY!

They've hit bumps along the way, needing new venues, new board members, new leadership. They've had conflict and people telling them they were wrong. That's the best news ever. Because as we know:

STEP 3: RESISTANCE IS ACCEPTABLE.

If not required. To bring it back to the world of video games: you always know you are going the right way when you are met with the most resistance.

OTHERS "PLAYING WITH COMMUNICATION"

People catch your eye. A person in a diner who stands out. An individual you shared an elevator with holds your attention. Someone who got out of the cab as you were getting in strikes an impression. Of the tens to hundreds of thousands of people you encounter, walk past, see, and become aware of in your life, a handful of them just "look" different. They "sound" different. Something about them "vibrates." Perhaps they are a point of gravity.

Maybe they have something special about them, maybe not. But even now, you can remember a handful of faces, people who stood out. I remember when I was a child seeing a woman driving a purple VW Bug, wearing a brown leather Daniel Boone jacket with a long fringe. Nothing special, but thirty-five years later, I remember her face.

Everyone I've talked to has a story like this.

My wife is practically a savant at seeing a random extra in a television show, with one awkwardly delivered line to a tertiary character and commenting, "(S)he's gonna be someone."

- She did this with Rami Malek in the early 2000s in his single scene in *Gilmore Girls* about "Assistant Pastor Erick."
- She noticed Natalie Dormer as the random extra in *Captain America.*
- Kristen Ritter, again in *Gilmore Girls.*
- Ellen Pompeo in *Friends.*

She can spot a "soon-to-be" better than anyone; it's a gift (until you watch TV with her).

Whether or not you have her near insane level of "called it," I'm willing to bet people/companies/brands jump out at and resonate with you.

Sometimes in a great way, others in a "steer clear" way. But "gravity" seems to be a "real" thing—if only in our perspective and perception.

THE BUSINESS WORLD ONLINE

Maybe you have a LinkedIn account, perhaps you don't. But LinkedIn has become a reputable force in the business world, attracting people from nearly every industry to share in a social media about advancing your career and cause. Unlike the vast array of other social media, LinkedIn keeps it fairly curated to business, which gives it a distinct vantage point of people's professional brand.

It allows for you to search people and companies in a way the old yellow pages only dreamed of.

(For the younger millennials and GenZ readers: the "yellow pages" was a big yellow book full of phone numbers of local businesses in your area, categorized by type, alphabetically. Like a large, clunky, semi-effective, analogue google. It also came in handy for a smaller person to sit taller at table or reach something off a slightly-too-tall shelf.)

Armed with my new perspective of "art," I started looking for communication ARTISTS. If art is "communication at play," I wanted to find people whose play … was communication.

I found some.

#JUSTQ AND THE URBAN MISFITS
Led by Quentin Allums with his hashtag #JustQ, the Urban Misfits are clearly playing with their communications, and they truly make a work of art. All the Misfits, including Eric Didier and Izzy Lugo III, are enigmatic, charismatic, and hard to take your eyes off.

Quentin is recognizable almost instantly, as his style and smile precede him. He is known for wearing a large black brimmed hat and greeting people with the Vulcan salute. He is a TEDx speaker, musician, producer, marketer, and entrepreneur. After only a year, Urban Misfit Ventures is taking off. It was accepted into the National Accelerator in Chicago, and Q was named on Wisconsin's 25 under 25. I'd say something smug here like, "He's so successful I hate him" ... except that, above all else, in our albeit brief interview, he came across as a truly nice and genuine individual.

He makes his art look fun, which I guess is the point.

Q IS A MUSICIAN

The world is full of people with that self-proclaimed moniker, from the substantial population of enthusiasts with a fender stack in their garage to marching bands and jazz ensembles across the nation. However, I've never heard anyone describe their process quite like him.

Making it in the world as a musician has a certain set of goals and obstacles. However, despite arguably constituting a "business," musical acts have a very different set of priorities than your average startup. For musicians, it's partly about your music, but also about your image, your vibe, your presence ... who YOU are. Where business has set supply lines and quantifiable metrics and measures to determine price and value, music is measured far beyond that to the qualifiable. "Sure, I like your music, but do I want to be your friend?"

MUSICIAN MEMORIES MISALIGNED

"I approach everything I'm doing like a musician: what does my brand feel like? What do I look like? How can I make people just addicted to me? ... When I create something, I want it to feel like a drug. What's that response that I want to elicit? How can I do that? So, I started testing things. I tried to tie my identity to Batman, I tried to tie it to wearing all black, I tried a Vulcan salute, the hat, implementing sound, all these different things that can elicit a response: 'Hey, he's talking—I need to listen.' And I rolled with what would stick, just like a musician."

Q's "gravity," although I'm pretty sure he wouldn't call it that, was intentional. It was tested, tried, altered, re-tested, and employed. When the world is full of people fighting over value and price, service and speed, Q made it about "the music." Making himself the voice and persona that quieted the crosstalk and got people to listen.

Paul and MagFest, programmers. Q, a musician ...

—JACKIE HERMES AT ACCELITY—

Accelity is a marketing agency in Milwaukee and is showing major growth, incredibly fast. But it started with Jackie as a one-woman show.

She was already working at a successful startup, a private equity SaaS company that was acquiring companies left and right and growing very fast. With each new acquisition, more resources went into sales. The company had upward of a hundred salespeople, but no marketing pipeline to speak of.

Jackie had ideas and experience she knew could add a lot of intelligence to the sales team, related to marketing automation and data insights. Ideas that today in 2020 we're familiar with. But these were new, scary, or at least unfamiliar terms, and the company wasn't interested in allocating resources toward making the salespeople smarter.

She saw the gravitational pull, so she started asking around. She reached out to some other startups to gauge interest and see their thoughts on the matter.

"They were really excited about it. ... If you can be smarter, as you sell as a startup, why wouldn't you want to do that, to get your revenue faster? ... It was a no-brainer."

The process started with just her, creating a pull and a force around something that people hadn't heard of and didn't understand. The private equity firm had its foot on the "sell, sell, sell" pedal and wasn't interested in marketing, especially something like "automated marketing" or any other "fad."

STEP 1: TAKE A STEP

Jackie started alone, just hustling to build up some steam. She worked with small companies and growing startups, using automation to add information that made companies smarter.

STEP 2: ADJUST AS NECESSARY

Jackie had her own brand of gravitational pull. She added the value, the access, and the personality to trust an as of yet untested market for some. She started small, grew slow, but the orbit took hold and now she's taking off.

STEP 3: RESISTANCE IS ACCEPTABLE

In a world of people looking for transactional relationships, "click now for the secret," Jackie releases free content, giving real guidance. In our phone call, she seemed very willing to tell me—or anyone, for that matter—her secrets. She's very willing to open up and give people anything they need.

Yes, there was pushback. Lots of it. But she creates an ecosystem of trust that shows to other people. It makes you trust her and her process. No smoke, no mirrors—a natural gravitational pull.

Media maven and utterly ineffable ...

SHAY ROWBOTTOM

When I first became aware of Rowbottom Media and Shay, it's actually a bit hard to describe.

Shay has a personality you have to see to understand. She's a bit more polarizing than Q, but love her or hate her, you'll find it hard to take your eyes off her. Her content, which not everyone likes, forces you to take notice and demands you have an opinion.

Aside from my interviewing her and discussing some of these topics with her personally, Shay has come up in multiple interviews, discussions, boards, panels, threads, or conversations I've had with other people.

I'll be very upfront: it isn't all positive. But critical, curious, or complimentary, I've yet to find the person who didn't have an opinion. She certainly forces a conversation, with her communication at play.

Her videos are energetic and fun. She does skits, poems, and enthusiastic tips. She offers value from a firehose. Not necessarily in the polished, "professional" manner that we expect from "business communications." But her take gets noticed, in a way that makes it hard to criticize its effectiveness.

The world is full of communicators and artists

WHY THEM?

For each of the four stories above, I found dozens more. Gravitational pulls from people approaching things in creative, over-the-top ways. As Troy said in the last chapter, when an innovator can break through a "no" wall with something different, they can generate a gravitational pull.

In a world of communications, these are examples of people who created an ecosystem. Their businesses are based off unexpected systems and approaches. After speaking with each of them, I can see why they shine. I can feel the gravity; I can see the Kreative emerging from the depths.

None used significant startup capital. None used an aggressive ad-buy or multipronged campaign. Just gravity, opportunity, and misaligned memories.

They took a step, they adjusted, they accepted resistance. But they also introduced their story with communication at play. This approach wasn't just business. No, it really was ART.

CHAPTER TWENTY-ONE

STICK THE LANDING

———

"Gymnastics tells you 'no' all day long. It mocks you over and over again, telling you that you're an idiot. That you're crazy. ... It's delicious. ... If you like falling, then gymnastics is the sport for you! You get to fall on your face, your ass, your back, your knees, and your pride! Good thing I didn't like falling ...

"I loved it!"

— MISSY PEREGRYM
AS HALEY GRAHAM
STICK IT, 2006

Everything in this book is wrong, or at least it will be. My perspectives expanded while writing the book, and I hope yours did reading it. Understanding, education, information, memories, experiences etc. are all fairly malleable, as they are based on a close to infinite number of factors up until that moment.

Everything in this book, to include the understanding, interpretations, and records of history, is up to change. Both my perspectives and the perspectives of the experts I interviewed for the book can and very probably will change.

Things change. The question is: what do we do when the things we know become incorrect, irrelevant, or outdated?

As the world moves on, grows, changes, and adapts to become only a shadow of the world we remember growing up in, do we change with it? Do we stand on traditions built in a world that has nothing to do with the one we live in?

Do we believe the media of the past and the memes of the present that paint a picture of a world that is ill-reflective of reality?

Do we suppress our ideas? Afraid that ignorance of a trend, or piece of data, or incorrect assumption will make us look stupid? Do we keep our head down and let the "leaders" take care of it?

Ummmm … no.

I hope this book is my biggest failure. The very best of my bad ideas. I am eager to learn what I didn't know. Where my perspective is woefully off, and where I may have found an opportunity through "the way it's done."

By laying out everything of who we are, we get to find out how wrong we are. We get new memories to misalign. New information. New perspectives.

Mistakes you made in your youth, adolescence, young adulthood, early career, etc. … they were mistakes, but they were based off your understanding, mind frame, and experience at the time. They were glorious mistakes. They lead you to where you are. Don't worry about past mess-ups, and don't be averse to messing up in the future, just see it as more opportunities.

The "History of Thinking" is continuing right now. New thought leadership, divergent understandings, new philosophies and outlooks on the world, business, problems and how to fix them. Success is the worst teacher there is. Some people get lucky, get rich, and coast on their perceived brilliance. They are rich, but they don't know as much as they think.

Failure is the actual teacher. You want success? Fail more.

History is full of people who have kept their ideas to themselves. You don't know their names, and neither do I. History is full of people who did an honest job, for an honest wage, worked their heart out and were miserable doing things they hated, but bowed to the requirements of "the real world" and "the way things work."

Other than relatives, you don't know those people either.

As we discussed in the very beginning, nonconformity in the modern era is discussed with an eye roll, as it has come to recognize a uniform, specific clique of nonconformity, the irony actually lost on those who include themselves. Books are written studying the nonconformist, narrating their habits and lifestyles as though it were an Animal Planet documentary narrating their mating or migratory habits.

The nonconformist is criticized for their "choices" to step out of society, but in my experience never congratulated for how hard they try to fit in when they think the whole of society is doing it wrong, but they go with the flow.

Nonconformity is backward. The nonconformists aren't the glam, goth, punk rockers, applying affectations of nonconformity to better fit as a standout from the norm. The nonconformist is the person truly incapable of fitting in, as "fit into what?" rings as their prevailing question.

In history, the nonconformists changed the way we thought, looked at a problem, or approached an issue. Those are the names that are remembered. Those are the people who change the world. Not many people could tell me the architect of the Notre Dame, or the Great Wall of China. Not many know who holds the record for the deepest dive into the Mariana Trench, or who holds the world record in the pole-vault. Who realized that silicon was an amazing insulator that made microchips work better and gave Silicon Valley its name?

I'm sure these things are Googleable. I'm also fairly confident, depending on your industry and background, you haven't heard of them.

But with Aristotle, Plato, Socrates, Newton, Archimedes, and the whole of the list in part one, whether or not you know why you know them, you remember their names because they added to our social and world UNDERSTANDING. They "invented" ways to think. That is innovation.

Building a better mousetrap may or may not be a great invention. If you follow the prescribed and described requirements inherent to the statement, you may or may not be successful. But you have a far better chance if you ignore the request and get to the requirements: less mice.

Give them what they need, almost never what they ask for. Don't build a better mousetrap; make friends with them mouse.

And when upon the torrent ocean of life you realize that the sea monster in your chest is unfed, unrecognized, and completely unheard, you will know that releasing your Kreative is the way to get yourself on course to the life you wanted to be living.

Release the Kreative! Let out the beast that is your perspective, your misaligned memories, your experiences and dreams. Don't hold back who you are or want to be because you are afraid of the opinions of those who aspire to mediocrity and hide in anonymity.

THE KRAKEN HAS NOTHING TO FEAR …

NEITHER DOES YOUR KREATIVE!

… To be continued

APPENDIX

ACKNOWLEDGMENTS

———

As I said in the Introduction:

I am not an anthropologist, psychologist, sociologist, or any other such "-ist" that would give me any particular credential, which is why I called every expert with a phone number to make sure I wasn't crazy before I wrote this book.

—ME, IN THE INTRODUCTION

For me, this book is far less an accomplishment of mine and more my gathering and assembling of the accomplishments of other people. Much like Edison, I didn't invent anything new here, just collected the brilliance of others and put my name on it.

Without the work of the people below, many of whom gave me time, opinions, redirection, advice (much of which I actually listened to), and a shoulder to cry on during my twice weekly authorial breakdowns, none of this would have happened.

To my team:

Natalie Westwood—My wife, who puts up with more than any three humans should have to.

Jeff Carpenter—My partner in various projects and "crimes" for over twenty years, who has been the grounding rod and cool head on strong shoulders that I never had.

Kory Arkwell—"My girl Friday," who kept the world moving and on track when I was forgetting to eat, sleep, move, drink water, or go home during the process of writing this book.

Nathaniel Olson—The sorcerer's apprentice. In so many ways I was only able to get this done because you were doing the stuff that needed doing.

Peter "Zeke" Dowty—Don't worry, I have a "Zeke" for that.

Kevin Crouch—You have fit into so many different categories of "lifesaver" in just the few short years I've known you. Thank you, for everything.

Ilia Epifanov—My Yoda and guide through the process. Thank you for liking my bad ideas and keeping me going.

To the people who offered their time, experience, and expertise to take my phone call, interview, or interjection into their life. Thank you so much for your expertise:

Frank Stephenson
Major General (RET) James
"Boe" Young
Carmen Simon
Troy DeVolld
Brandon Sawyer
Quentin Allums
Shay Rowbottom
Jackie Hermes
Paul Good

Adam Carter
Megan Taylor
Peter Thaxter
Glenn Croston
Denise Gosnell
Luke Marlowe
Georgetown Philosophy
Department
MagFest Board
of Directors

To my community and friends who offered their thoughts, ideas, guidance, and expertise to put me back on track as I let my mind wander:

Emily Ricotta
Elena Artimovich
Greg Westwood
Rachel Westwood
John Westwood
Nate Westwood
Cassi Willard

And to everyone who read this book, laughed at the jokes, and found they wanted to release the Kreative.

APPENDIX

BIBLIOGRAPHY

———

INTRODUCTION

Caroline Frost, "Jack Ma, The Richest Man in China, Stepped Down as Alibaba Chairman—Markets Insider." 2019 Makets.Businessinsider.Com. https://markets.businessinsider.com/news/stocks/jack-ma-quotes-alibaba-inspirational-2019-6-1028295089.

Drucker, Peter Ferdinand. 1999. Landmarks of Tomorrow. New Brunswick: Transaction Publishers.

Eliot, T. S. (1934), The Rock, London: Faber & Faber

CHAPTER 1

Annamarya Scaccia "Hippopotomonstroses-Quippedaliophobia: What Is It?." 2020. Healthline. https://www.healthline.com/health/hippopotomonstrosesquippedaliophobia.

Barrow, Clyde W. "*More than a historian: the political and economic thought of Charles A. Beard*," Transaction Publishers, 2000.

Beard, Charles "The Economic Interpretation of the Constitution of the United States" 1913

Beard, Charles A. Written History as an Act of Faith – 1933

"Charles A. Beard Biography," American Historical Association, 2020, Accessed Jan 19, 2020

Croston, Glenn "The Real Story of Risk" Prometheus 2012

Drake, Richard "Charles Austin Beard: The Return of the Master Historian of American Imperialism". Cornell University Press. Retrieved August 9, 2019

"Glossophobia (Fear of Public Speaking): Are You Glossophobic?" 2020. Psycom.Net - Mental Health Treatment Resource

"Human Shark Bait." 2020. National Geographic - Videos, TV Shows & Photos - Canada. http://natgeotv.com/ca/human-shark-bait/facts.

"Seat Belts." 2016. NHTSA. https://www.nhtsa.gov/risky-driving/seat-belts.

Steimer, Thierry. 2002. "The Biology of Fear- and Anxiety-Related Behaviors." Dialogues in Clinical Neuroscience 4 (3): 231. https://www.ncbi.nlm.nih.gov/pmc/articles/PMC3181681

Since 1986. https://www.psycom.net/glossophobia-fear-of-public-speaking.

Seinfeld, Jerry 'I'm Telling you for the Last Time' 1998

Troncale, Joseph "Your Lizard Brain." 2020. Psychology Today. https://www.psychologytoday.com/us/blog/where-addiction-meets-your-brain/201404/your-lizard-brain.

"Venomous Snake Faqs." 2020. Ufwildlife.Ifas.Ufl.Edu. https://ufwildlife.ifas.ufl.edu/venomous_snake_faqs.shtml.

"Which New Schooler Are You Most Like?." 2020. The New School. https://www.newschool.edu/about/history/.

CHAPTER 2

"A.N Whitehead on Plato" The Core Curriculum, Columbia College, Accessed Jan 22, 2020

Kraut, Richard "Plato," *The Stanford Encyclopedia of Philosophy* (Fall 2017 Edition), Edward N. Zalta

Nails, Debra "Socrates," *The Stanford Encyclopedia of Philosophy* (Spring 2020 Edition), Edward N. Zalta (ed.),

Shields, Christopher "Aristotle," *The Stanford Encyclopedia of Philosophy* (Winter 2016 Edition), Edward N. Zalta (ed.),

CHAPTER 3

Alban, Francis Bacon, Viscount St (1 January 1620), "Instauratio magna preliminaries," in Rees (ed.), The Oxford Francis Bacon, Vol. 11: The Instauratio magna Part II: Novum organum and Associated Texts, Oxford University Press, pp. 2–495

Andrews, Bill "5 Times Einstein Was Wrong," Astronomy.com, 2018 retrieved Jan 25, 2020

Angelo, Megan, "16 Unforgettable Things Maya Angelou Wrote and said," Glamour 2014

Brewton, Sue "Squire Bill Widener vs Theodore Roosevelt" 2014

Buchanan, Mark "Why Einstein Was Wrong About Relativity." 2008, accessed Jan 10, 2020

Comins, Neil F "Discovering the Essential Universe" p.27 W.H. Freeman, 2012

Dolnick, Edward - The Clockwork Universe: Isaac Newton, Royal Society, and the Birth of the Modern World, Harper Collins 2011

Fellows Directory - Royal Society." Royalsociety.org. Retrieved 1 June 2019.

Hood, John "Chariots of Fire," National Review 2008, Accessed Jan 07, 2020

"Isaac Newton's Lost Alchemy Recipe Rediscovered, National Geographic 2016, retrieved Jan 7, 2020

Letzter, Rafi "Hidden Gravitational Wave Signal Reveals That Black Holes Are 'Bald'" LiveScience, 2019

Meyer, Susan "Leaders of the Scientific Revolution: Isaac Newton" p.22 Rosen Publishing Group 2018

Mikkelson, David "Are U.S. Railroad Gauges Based on Roman Chariots?" Snopes 2001, accessed Jan 07, 2020

Roosevelt, Theodore "Theodore Roosevelt: An Autobiography" p. 337 Charles Scribner's Sons, 1920

"The Formal Title as Adopted in the Royal Charter" 1663 royalsociety.org, Accessed Jan 03, 2020

"This Day in History: Isaac Newton is Knighted". History Channel. A&E Television Networks. 20 June 2016. Retrieved August 23, 2020.

Thompson, Hobie and Havern, Sarah "The History of Gravity" Stanford.edu, retrieved Jan 21, 2020

Thompson, Avery "Scientists Rule Out Hawking Theory for Source of Dark Matter," Popular Mechanics, 2019

Weisman, Steven R. "Daniel Patrick Moynihan: A Portrait in Letters of an America Visionary, Moynihan Estate 2010

Zyga, Lisa "What Happen when Newton's third law is broken?" Phys.Org, 2015

CHAPTER 4

Berkun, Scott "The Myths of Innovation" ch. 5, O'Reilly, 2010

Cook, Mariana "Mathematicians: An Outer View of the Inner World" p.76, American Mathematical Society 2018

Strauss, Valerie "American schools are modeled after factories and treat students like widgets. Right? Wrong." Washington Post, 2015

Weiner, Ben. 2018. "Why the U.S. Has a STEM Shortage and How We Fix it (Part 1) > Recruiting News and Views @ Recruitingdaily." Recruiting News and Views @ Recruitingdaily. https://recruitingdaily.com/why-the-u-s-has-a-stem-shortage-and-how-we-fix-it-part-1/.

CHAPTER 5

"1893: Edison Records First Sneeze on Film" APS.org 2001, accessed Jan 11, 2020

Cugnot, Nicolas-Joseph Brittanica.com retrieved Jan 20, 2020

Daimler, AG "The birth of the automobile." Archived from the original on 21 November 2015. Retrieved 1 October 2014

Flink, James The Automobile Idea. (1990). MIT Press. p. 5.

"How Ford Is Innovating with Materials Science." 2020. Fortune.

"History of the Lightbulb" Energy.gov, retrieved Jan 25, 2020

"Henry Ford," Biography 2019, Accessed on Jan 11, 2020

"Henry Ford - Visionaries on Innovation - The Henry Ford." 2020. Thehenryford.Org.

Ransom E. Olds, Automotive Hall of fame 2020, Automotivehalloffame.org

"The Long Shop Museum » Richard Garrett And Sons." 2020. Longshopmuseum.Co.Uk.

"The Model T | Johns Hopkins University Press Books." 2020. Jhupbooks.Press.Jhu.Edu.

"Thomas Edison Patented the Kinetoscope" America's Story, from America's Library, accessed Jan 20, 2020

CHAPTER 5

"Best-Selling Book." 2020. Guinness World Records.

"How the Oldest Depiction of Sex Changed the Way We See the Ancient Egyptians." 2019. Culturacolectiva.Com.

"Phoenicians: Sailing Away [Ushistory.Org]." 2020. Ushistory.Org.

CHAPTER 6

BBC Wales, "Marconi's Waves." Archived from the original on 20 January 2007. Retrieved 20 January 2007

Cognitive Science (Stanford Encyclopedia of Philosophy)." 2020. Plato.Stanford.Edu.

"Cognitive Science - An Overview | Sciencedirect Topics." 2020. Sciencedirect.Com.

"History of Technology - From the Middle Ages to 1750." 2020. Encyclopedia Britannica.

Kretschmann HJ, et al. 2020. "Human Brain Growth in the 19Th and 20Th Century. - PubMed - NCBI." Ncbi.Nlm.Nih.Gov.

Muybridge, Eadweard; Mozley, Anita Ventura (foreword) (1887). Muybridge's Complete Human and Animal Locomotion: All 781 Plates from the 1887 Animal Locomotion. Courier Dover Publications. p. xvii.

Schatzkin, Paul (2002), The Boy Who Invented Television. Silver Spring, Maryland: Teamcom Books, p. 50.

CHAPTER 7

BBC Wales, "Marconi's Waves." *Archived from the* original *on 20 January 2007.* Retrieved 20 January 2007

Cognitive Science (Stanford Encyclopedia of Philosophy)." 2020. Plato.Stanford.Edu.

"Cognitive Science - An Overview | Sciencedirect Topics." 2020. Sciencedirect.Com.

"History of Technology - From the Middle Ages to 1750." 2020. Encyclopedia Britannica.

Kretschmann HJ, et al. 2020. "Human Brain Growth in the 19Th and 20Th Century. - PubMed - NCBI." Ncbi.Nlm.Nih.Gov.

Muybridge, Eadweard; Mozley, Anita Ventura (foreword) (1887). Muybridge's Complete Human and Animal Locomotion: All 781 Plates from the 1887 Animal Locomotion. Courier Dover Publications. p. xvii.

Schatzkin, Paul (2002), The Boy Who Invented Television. Silver Spring, Maryland: Teamcom Books, p. 50.

CHAPTER 8

"Build a Better Mousetrap." 2011. National Museum of American History.

CHAPTER 9

Nicholas Meyer, William Shatner, Leonard Nimoy, Kirstie Alley (1982). Star Trek II: The Wrath of Khan (DVD). Paramount.

CHAPTER 10

"As Game Boy Turns 30, It's Time to Recognize Its Inventor, Nintendo's Maintenance Man." 2020. Fortune.

"Console Gaming Then and Now: A Fascinating 1997 Interview with Nintendo's Legendary Gunpei Yokoi." 2015. TechSpot.

"Gunpei Yokoi." 2020. Nintendo.

"Gunpei Yokoi, Chief Designer of Game Boy, Is Dead at 56." 2020. Nytimes.Com.

CHAPTER 11

Boeriu, Horatiu. 2012. "The History of the MINI Cooper." BMW BLOG.

English, Trevor, Brown, Ariella and McFadden, Christopher. 2017. "The History and Evolution of the Wheel."

Interestingengineering.Com.

Gambino, Megan 2009. "A Salute to the Wheel." Smithsonian Magazine.

"History of MINI – Story, Heritage & Origins – MINI USA." 2020. MINIUSA.

"Invention of the Wheel - Timeline Index." 2020. Timelineindex.Com.

"The Wheel Timeline.." 2020. Timetoast.

Trotta, Mark. 2020. "Classic Mini History." Classic-Car-History.Com.

Wolchover, Natalie 2012. "Why It Took So Long to Invent the Wheel." Livescience.Com.

CHAPTER 12

"History of An Icon: Fiat 500." 2020. ITALY Magazine.

History of the Fiat Panda - Part 2: First Series." 2018. DriveTribe.

Original Influencer: The History of the Lamborghini Miura | Automobile Magazine - Automobile." 2019. Automobile.

Scottsdale, FIAT. 2020. "FIAT 500 | History of The FIAT 500 | In Scottsdale and Near Phoenix, AZ." Fiatusaofscottsdale.Com.

CHAPTER 13

"About Charter Schools | National Alliance for Public Charter Schools." 2020. National Alliance for Public Charter Schools.

Budde, Ray. 1988. "Education by Charter: Restructuring School Districts. Key to Long-Term Continuing Improvement in American Education." Publication Sales, Regional Laboratory for Educational Improvement of the Northeast and Islands

"Everybody Is A Genius. But If You Judge a Fish by Its Ability to Climb a Tree, It Will Live Its Whole Life Believing That It Is Stupid – Quote Investigator." 2020. Quoteinvestigator.Com.

"History and Applications - The Newton–Leibniz Controversy." 2020. Amsi.Org.Au.

"Leibniz - The Story of Mathematics - A History of Mathematical Thought from Ancient Times to the Modern Day." 2020.

"NCSRC | National Charter School Resource Center." 2020. Charterschoolcenter. Ed.Gov. https://charterschoolcenter.ed.gov/what-charter-school.

Peterson, Paul. 2010. "No, Al Shanker Did Not Invent the Charter School - Education Next." Education Next.

Schroeder, Joy 2004, "Ripples of Innovation: Charter Schooling in Minnesota, the nation's first charter school state" Progressive Policy Institute

Seth Godin "Education Needs to Be Inconvenient." 2018. Seth's Blog.

Seth Godin "School Is Still Ruining Your Chances to Learn." 2017. Medium.

"STOP STEALING DREAMS: Seth Godin at TEDxYouth@BFS." 2020. YouTube.

"Summit Public Schools." 2020. Summitps.Org.

"Summit Preparatory Charter High." 2019. U.S. News Report. Accessed Dec 09, 2019

"Who Invented Calculus - Newton or Leibniz? Learn the History of Calculus." 2016. The Great Courses Daily.

"Why Do So Many Parents Opt Out of Summit Learning? | Elearninginside News." 2018. Elearninginside News. https://news.elearninginside.com/why-do-so-many-parents-opt-out-of-summit-learning/.

CHAPTER 14

"75Th Innovation CMD." 2020. Usar.Army.Mil.

Judson, Jen, and Jen Judson. 2019. "Army Futures Command Is Ready for Prime Time." Defense News.

Chapter 15

Gates, Bill "Business @ The Speed of Thought" 1999, Management Paradise

"History Faceoff: Who Was First in Flight?." 2020. HISTORY.

"Steve Jobs Stanford Commencement Speech 2005." 2020. YouTube.

"The Condiment Mustard's History." 2020. The Spruce Eats. https://www.thespruceeats.com/history-of-mustard-as-food-1807631.

"The History of Dijon Mustard." 2020. Kitchenproject.Com. https://kitchenproject.com/history/Dijon-Mustard/index.htm.

"The Only Reason the Mac Looks Like It Does Is Because Steve Jobs Dropped in on a Course Taught by This Former Monk." 2020. Business Insider

Who Is Credited with Inventing the Telephone?" 2020. The Library of Congress.

"Why Steve Jobs Drowned the First iPod Prototype | Cult of Mac." 2014. Cult of Mac.

CHAPTER 16

Doss, Henry. 2020. "Innovation: A Tale of Language, Marissa Mayer, Francis Bacon and the Sonnet." Forbes.

Ghose, Tia. 2012. "Most Ocean Species Remain Undiscovered." Livescience.Com.

Marshall, Carrie, and MacFormat 265. 2013. "The Appleseed Legend: The Story Behind Apple's Unofficial Mascot." TechRadar.

"The Real-Life Origins of the Legendary Kraken." 2015. The Conversation. https://theconversation.com/the-real-life-origins-of-the-legendary-kraken-52058.

Zipkin, Nina. 2016. "16 Inspirational Quotes from Walt

CHAPTER 17

"Ceylon Vs. Cassia — Not All Cinnamon Is Created Equal." 2020. Healthline

Coleman, Liz. 2020. "A Call to Reinvent Liberal Arts Education." Ted.Com.

CHAPTER 18

Cooper, Alan "The Inmates are Running the Asylum" 1999 Sams

"Personas – A Simple Introduction." 2020. The Interaction Design Foundation.

"The Origin of Personas." 2008. Cooper. https://www.cooper.com/journal/2008/05/the_origin_of_personas/.

Chapter 19

"Interview with Donald Trump." 2016. The Daily News.

"Jon Stewart On Crossfire." 2020. YouTube.